SPECTRUM
Science
Test Practice

Grade 8

Published by
Frank Schaffer Publications®

Editor: Karen Thompson

Frank Schaffer Publications®

Send all inquiries to:
Frank Schaffer Publications
8720 Orion Place
Columbus, Ohio 43240-2111

Science Test Practice—grade 8

ISBN 0-7696-8068-2

3 4 5 6 7 8 9 MAZ 11 10 09 08 07

SCIENCE TEST PRACTICE
Table of Contents
Grade 8

SCIENCE TEST PRACTICE
Table of Contents
Grade 8

ABOUT THIS BOOK

Science Test Practice is for everyone who wants to have a working knowledge of the fundamentals of science. Written with the goal of helping students achieve on science tests, it approaches science through the format of the National Science Education Standards.

The National Science Education Standards were developed by the National Academy of Science, an organization of the leading scientists in the United States. Their goal is for all students to achieve scientific literacy. To be scientifically literate means to be able to understand the richness of the world around us; to be able to make decisions based on the skills and processes that science teaches us; and to approach problems and challenges creatively.

This book is divided into four sections, each one based on a National Science Education Content Standard. This book focuses on content standards A-D: Science as Inquiry, Physical Science, Life Science, and Earth and Space Science, with one section devoted to each standard. Standards E-G, which cover science and technology and science in personal and social perspectives, are covered within the four sections. A correlation chart details the coverage of all standards in the book (see pp. 7-8).

How to Use the Book

Students can begin with the Pretest (pp. 9-14). This test covers all the three major strands of science:

- physical science, which includes how objects move and interact;

- life science, which includes animals, plants, and ecosystems;

- earth and space science, which includes rocks and minerals, the oceans, and the solar system.

After the Pretest, you may wish to complete the test prep practice in order, or complete the sections out of sequence. Before completing the practice pages, students should read *Hints and Strategies for Answering Questions* on page 6.

Finally, the Posttest (pp. 86-91) gives students a chance to practice yet again, applying the knowledge gleaned from the rest of the book. A complete answer key appears at the back of the book.

With its real-life questions and standards-based approach, *Science Test Practice* will engage students; give them solid test-taking hints and practice; and provide them an opportunity to build their confidence for other exams.

Multiple Choice

When you encounter a multiple-choice item, read the question carefully until you are sure of its meaning. After reading the question, read all answer choices carefully. Remember that only one answer is absolutely correct; this will be the one that appears to be the truest. Rule out the answer choices that are obviously wrong and choose the answer that holds true for the science scenario, based on what you have studied. Sometimes you will need to refer to a passage or diagram to find the information you need.

Fill-in-the-Blank

When you have to fill in the blanks in a sentence, paragraph, or diagram, read the entire item carefully. Then read it a second time, pausing to think about the missing words or phrases. You can then begin to plug in the words of which you are certain. If you are not sure about a word or phrase, look for clues in other words of the sentence or paragraph. If a Word Bank is provided, cross out each word as you use it. Remember that the missing words or phrases must agree with the articles and verbs in the sentence.

Short Response

A short response answer usually includes three to four sentences. When you encounter a short response item, read the question carefully. If necessary, return to a passage or diagram to find relevant information. When you are ready to respond, try to think about one topic sentence that can summarize your answer. Write it down, then add two or three sentences that support your topic sentence.

Extended Response

An extended response, or essay, includes three parts: an introduction where you state your main idea or position, a body where you add details that support your topic idea, and a conclusion where you summarize your topic idea. When you have to write an extended response, read the question carefully. Decide whether you have to write a narrative based on a passage or diagram, or argue your point of view on a subject. Then write an introductory paragraph that explains the topic you want to discuss. In the body of the essay, try to be clear and concise, including only information that is necessary and supports the topic.

CORRELATIONS TO STANDARDS

National Science Education Content Standards Correlation

As a result of activities in grades 5-8, all students should develop an understanding of the concepts below.

Standard	Pages
CONTENT STANDARD A: Science as inquiry	
Abilities necessary to do scientific inquiry	15-25
To learn about the world in a scientific manner, students need to learn how to ask questions, formulate possible answers, devise experiments to test those answers, and base their conclusions on evidence.	
Understanding about scientific inquiry	26-29
Students need to understand that the investigations used to gather information depend on the question being asked; that scientists use mathematics and technology as they work; and that scientists build on the work other scientists have done, by asking questions about that work and that grow out of that work.	
CONTENT STANDARD B: Physical Science	
Properties and changes of properties in matter	27, 32-37
Motion and forces	38-40
Transfer of energy	27, 41-45
CONTENT STANDARD C: Life Science	
Structure and function in living systems	46-51, 53, 67, 68
Reproduction and heredity	48, 52-57
Regulation and behavior	61, 62, 66
Populations and ecosystems	57, 58-62
Diversity and adaptations of organisms	66-70
CONTENT STANDARD D: Earth and Space Science	
Structure of the earth system	71-80
Earth's history	26, 35, 70, 73, 74
Earth in the solar system	81-85

National Science Education Content Standards Correlation

CONTENT STANDARD E: Science and Technology	
Abilities of technological design	27, 30, 31
Understanding about science and technology	27, 30, 31

CONTENT STANDARD F: Science in Personal and Social Perspectives	
Science can seem removed from everyday life, but it actually surrounds us. Personal hygiene activities are based on scientific reasoning. Understanding the risks and benefits in the world makes students more informed citizens.	
Personal health	64, 65
Populations, resources, and environments	26, 61-62, 66
Natural hazards	63
Risks and benefits	26, 31, 64, 65
Science and technology in society	30, 31

CONTENT STANDARD G: History and Nature of Science	
Science as a human endeavor	30, 31, 35, 42, 58, 65, 69
Science is a pursuit of human beings, with many different skills, backgrounds, qualities, and talents. However, scientists all share curiosity about the world, a tendency to ask questions about what is known, an openness to new ideas, insight, and creativity.	
Nature of science	16, 17, 23-25, 26, 27, 28, 29, 42, 46, 65, 68
History of science	16, 25, 65, 69, 75, 81

Grade 8 Pretest

Directions: Read the questions. Choose the truest possible answer.

1. Shakira wants to know which location in her apartment is best for growing African violets. She has three African violets. She puts one on the balcony, one by the kitchen window, and one on the mantel in the living room. Each plant has the same size pot and the same soil, and Shakira gives each plant the same amount of water. In this experiment, what is the independent variable?

   (A) type of plant
   (B) type of soil
   (C) plant location
   (D) amount of water

2. Trevor wants to find out how temperature affects plant growth. He thinks that warmer temperatures will promote faster plant growth. Trevor stores four plants of the same type in locations with different temperatures. He controls all the other variables. Trevor records the growth of each plant every week for two months. What is the next step Trevor should take?

   (F) analyze his data
   (G) test his hypothesis
   (H) identify the problem
   (J) form his hypothesis

3. Latoya thinks her kindergarten students might learn to read faster if she uses a teaching method focused on the sounds different letters make. For two months, she teaches half of her class using this method. She keeps teaching the other half of the class by reading aloud with them. What is the control in this study?

   (A) the two-month time period
   (B) the students Latoya reads to
   (C) the students Latoya teaches about letter sounds
   (D) the number of new words the students learn to read

4. The particles in motion around the nucleus of a carbon-12 atom are called _____ .

   (F) quarks
   (G) protons
   (H) neutrons
   (J) electrons

5. Carbon-14 differs from carbon-12 in terms of _____ .

   (A) atomic number
   (B) number of protons
   (C) number of neutrons
   (D) number of electrons

6. Which type of element is sodium?

   (F) halogen
   (G) noble gas
   (H) alkali metal
   (J) alkaline earth metal

GO ON

7. Which of the following scenarios does *not* involve a chemical change?

   (A) melting ice

   (B) frying eggs

   (C) burning wood

   (D) rusting metal

8. How is a gas different from a liquid or solid?

   (F) The particles in a gas are closer together.

   (G) The particles in a gas move more slowly.

   (H) Both liquids and solids have definite volumes.

   (J) Substances can move between liquid and solid states.

9. Your family is driving to Atlanta for your grandparents' 50th wedding anniversary. If you live 800 miles from Atlanta, and your average driving speed is 60 mph, about how long will the drive take?

   (A) 5 hours

   (B) 8 hours

   (C) 13 hours

   (D) 26 hours

10. While riding her bicycle, your little sister goes from a full stop to 9 m/s in 3 minutes. How fast is she accelerating?

   (F) 3.0 m/s

   (G) 3.0 m/s^2

   (H) 1.5 m/s

   (J) 1.5 m/s^2

11. Which quality affects an object's inertia?

   (A) its mass

   (B) whether or not it is moving

   (C) how much friction it encounters

   (D) the direction in which it is moving

12. Tai's little brother Gan weighs 15 kg. His swing weighs 2 kg. How much force will Tai need to use to push Gan on the swing to make Gan accelerate at 4 m/s^2?

   (F) 4 N

   (G) 12 N

   (H) 60 N

   (J) 68 N

13. When a car skids on ice, what kind of friction is acting on the wheels?

   (A) cold friction

   (B) static friction

   (C) sliding friction

   (D) rolling friction

14. When Raquel jumps up to make a basket, which force returns her to the ground?

   (F) mass

   (G) inertia

   (H) gravity

   (J) friction

GO ON

15. A rainbow is produced when light waves change speed as they pass through water droplets into air. This process is called _____ .

- (A) diffraction
- (B) refraction
- (C) reflection
- (D) interference

16. Which of the following sentences about minerals is true?

- (F) Minerals are liquids at room temperature.
- (G) Minerals are organic compounds.
- (H) Minerals are always artificially created.
- (J) Minerals have a definite chemical composition.

17. The Mohs scale is used to compare minerals in terms of their _____ .

- (A) streak
- (B) luster
- (C) hardness
- (D) cleavage

18. What causes the red color of a ruby?

- (F) chromium
- (G) zinc
- (H) bauxite
- (J) titanium

19. In X-ray crystallography, a crystal diffracts X-rays in a characteristic pattern. Which characteristic of the crystalline substance is this process used to determine?

- (A) age
- (B) purity
- (C) specific gravity
- (D) atomic structure

20. When some volcanoes erupt, they eject molten material that later cools, forming rocks. Which type of rock is formed by this process?

- (F) igneous
- (G) organic
- (H) metamorphic
- (J) sedimentary

21. Shells of mussels, clams, corals, and snails gather on the ocean floor. Over time they solidify into rock. Which type of rock is formed by this process?

- (A) intrusive igneous
- (B) extrusive igneous
- (C) organic sedimentary
- (D) nonfoliated metamorphic

GO ON

Name_____ Date_____

22. **Which geologic features are formed when two continental plates collide?**
    - (F) islands
    - (G) canyons
    - (H) mountains
    - (J) rift valleys

23. **What causes earthquakes?**
    - (A) sections of rock breaking apart
    - (B) tsunamis forming underwater
    - (C) upwellings of magma underneath the continental plates
    - (D) plates of Earth's crust colliding with plates of the upper mantle

24. **Mount St. Helens, which erupted violently in 1980, is a composite volcano. Which of the following did its eruption release?**
    - (F) ash
    - (G) lava
    - (H) rocks
    - (J) cinders

25. **What is a gene?**
    - (A) a section of DNA that codes for a protein
    - (B) a molecule found in the backbone of DNA
    - (C) a part of DNA that codes for a trait, such as skin color
    - (D) a molecule found on the rungs of the DNA ladder

26. **How does phenotype differ from genotype?**
    - (F) Phenotype is observable.
    - (G) Genotype changes over time.
    - (H) Phenotype determines gender.
    - (J) Genotype is affected by heredity.

27. **White fur is recessive in mice. If both parents have white fur, what is the likelihood that one of their offspring will have white fur?**
    - (A) 25%
    - (B) 50%
    - (C) 75%
    - (D) 100%

28. **Female elephants prefer mates with larger tusks. According to the principle of natural selection, which of the following will occur over time?**
    - (F) Female elephants will bear fewer young.
    - (G) The preferences of female elephants will change.
    - (H) The less desirable trait will begin to disappear in male elephants.
    - (J) Male elephants will begin to fight each other to win mates.

29. **What can scientists tell from the amount of carbon-14 in a human bone?**
    - (A) how old the bone is
    - (B) where the bone was buried
    - (C) whether the person was poisoned
    - (D) whether the person was a man or a woman

GO ON

30. **Which of the following organisms appeared first in geologic time?**

    (F) fish

    (G) mice

    (H) humans

    (J) crocodiles

31. **Which gas is most common in Earth's atmosphere?**

    (A) oxygen

    (B) nitrogen

    (C) water vapor

    (D) carbon dioxide

32. **How is air in high mountains different from air at sea level?**

    (F) The air in the mountains is warmer.

    (G) The air in the mountains is less dense.

    (H) The air at sea level contains more ozone.

    (J) The air at sea level can carry radio waves.

33. **The ozone layer is beneficial to human health because it _____.**

    (A) absorbs chlorofluorocarbons

    (B) serves as a source of oxygen

    (C) protects the Earth against meteors

    (D) shields us from the full force of the sun

34. **Clouds are formed by which process?**

    (F) conduction

    (G) evaporation

    (H) precipitation

    (J) condensation

35. **Many scientists have linked rising global temperatures to an increase in _____.**

    (A) ozone

    (B) fishing

    (C) plant matter

    (D) carbon dioxide

36. **Why may shark meat contain toxic substances used in pesticides?**

    (F) because sharks are plant eaters

    (G) because sharks have highly absorbent skin

    (H) because sharks are bred near human habitation

    (J) because sharks eat fish that eat plants

37. **Why does paving land for parking lots and highways increase the risk of flooding?**

    (A) Asphalt absorbs heat.

    (B) Water can't soak into the pavement.

    (C) Car emissions increase rainfall.

    (D) Parking lots and highways prevent evaporation.

38. **During the process of phytoremediation, plants _____.**

    (F) prevent erosion of landfills

    (G) block nutrient runoff

    (H) create gasoline from garbage

    (J) absorb metals from contaminated soil

GO ON

39. **Which of the following is the smallest organizational level in the human body?**

    Ⓐ cell

    Ⓑ organ

    Ⓒ tissue

    Ⓓ muscle

40. **What is the primary function of the kidneys?**

    Ⓕ digesting food

    Ⓖ removing waste

    Ⓗ producing energy

    Ⓙ regulating respiration

41. **Why do we see only one side of the moon?**

    Ⓐ The moon is only visible at night.

    Ⓑ The sun only lights one side of the moon.

    Ⓒ The shadow of the earth blocks the other side of the moon.

    Ⓓ The rotation and orbit of the moon take the same amount of time.

42. **Which of the following planets is closest to the earth?**

    Ⓕ Mars

    Ⓖ Saturn

    Ⓗ Mercury

    Ⓙ Neptune

43. **Before the 1500s, most people believed the center of the universe was _____.**

    Ⓐ the sun

    Ⓑ Earth

    Ⓒ the moon

    Ⓓ a black hole

44. **What causes a star to shine?**

    Ⓕ reflected light from the sun

    Ⓖ energy released from the fusion of hydrogen atoms

    Ⓗ a collapse of the core to the point that it has no volume

    Ⓙ gradual combustion of the elements making up the core

45. **During lab work, you should wear a thermal mitt when _____.**

    Ⓐ working with a strong acid

    Ⓑ heating a solution on a hot plate

    Ⓒ dissecting something using a scalpel

    Ⓓ working with something that might stain your hands

46. **Which best explains why broken thermometers are dangerous?**

    Ⓕ Mercury is highly toxic.

    Ⓖ The contents evaporate rapidly.

    Ⓗ It is easy to cut yourself on broken glass.

    Ⓙ The substances inside thermometers degrade unpredictably.

Name_____   Date_____

════════════════════ **Grade 8** ════════════════════

Directions: Identify each safety symbol shown below.

Directions: Read each question. Write your answers on the lines provided.

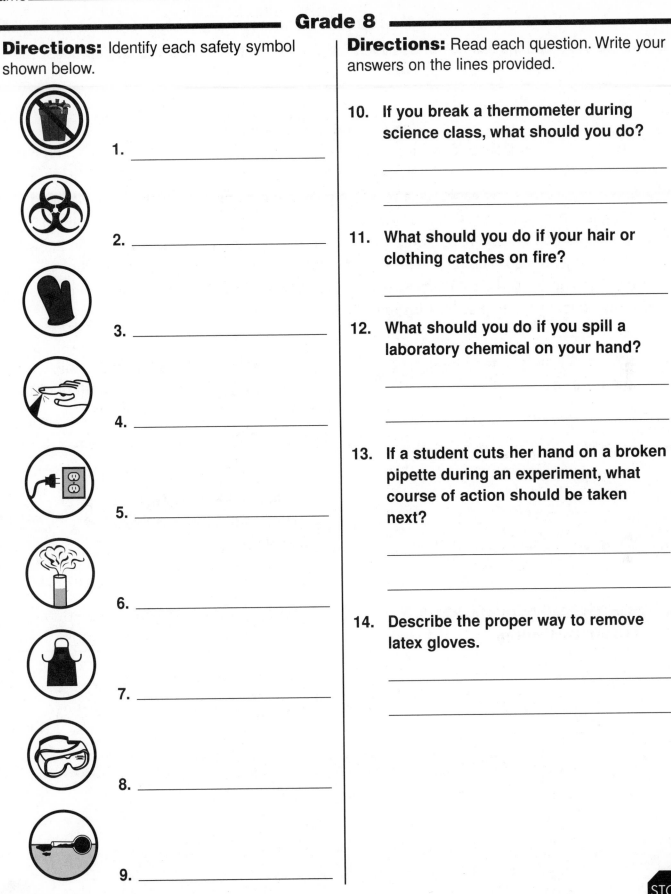

1. _____

2. _____

3. _____

4. _____

5. _____

6. _____

7. _____

8. _____

9. _____

10. If you break a thermometer during science class, what should you do?

_____

_____

11. What should you do if your hair or clothing catches on fire?

_____

12. What should you do if you spill a laboratory chemical on your hand?

_____

_____

13. If a student cuts her hand on a broken pipette during an experiment, what course of action should be taken next?

_____

_____

14. Describe the proper way to remove latex gloves.

_____

_____

STOP

0-7696-8068-2—*Science Test Practice*

Grade 8

Directions: Read the text below. Use information from the text to help you answer questions 1–6.

Rock and Roll Insulation

Kate plays bass in a band. The band practices in the garage adjacent to her house, and her parents have begun to complain about the noise. Kate's parents want the band to practice elsewhere, but there is no space available at the other band members' houses. Kate wants to know how she can best block the noise. She finds three different types of insulation and puts them on the garage walls. She puts blankets on one wall, cardboard with spray foam on another wall, and fiberglass insulation on a third wall. She does not cover the wall containing the automatic garage door. Then she asks the singer to go listen from outside each wall while the rest of the band members play their instruments.

1. **What will Kate ask the singer when she returns?**

   _____

2. **What is the independent variable in this experiment?**

   _____

3. **What is the dependent variable?**

   _____

4. **Name one problem with Kate's experimental design.**

   _____

   _____

5. **Name one factor, other than noise-blocking properties, that Kate might want to consider in choosing insulation.**

   _____

6. **What will Kate probably do after finding out the results of her experiment?**

   _____

   _____

   _____

Name_____ Date_____

Directions: Read the following text and fill in the blanks with words from the Word Bank. Some words may be used more than once.

Word Bank

one	light	light level	seed germination	in the closet	highest
medium	hypothesize	sprout	bar graph	germination	seeds

Ms. Meyer's science class is studying seed germination and seedling growth. Each team of students is testing one factor to see how it affects these processes. The students are careful to change **1.** _____ factor at a time so they will know what causes differences in their results.

For example, Le Mei and Kevin are studying the affect of **2.** _____ on germination. They are comparing three pots, each containing five seeds. One pot is in a dark closet, one is under fluorescent lights 24 hours a day, and the third is in a windowsill. They will compare the two pots exposed to light to the pot in the closet. The independent variable is **3.** _____ , while the dependent variable is **4.** _____ . The pot **5.** _____ serves as the control, while the other two act as the experimental groups.

The pot with the **6.** _____ level of **7.** _____ is the one under the lamps. The pot in the closet gets no light. The pot with the **8.** _____ level is the one on the windowsill. Le Mei and Kevin **9.** _____ that the pot under the fluorescent light will sprout before the one on the windowsill. They will observe the pots for three weeks and record the number of seeds that **10.** _____ in each group. They will also record how long the seeds take to sprout.

To present their results to the class, they will organize the data using a **11.** _____ . The results will indicate how much light is best for seed **12.** _____ . To expand their experiment, Le Mei and Kevin might want to use different kinds of **13.** _____ and greater levels of **14.** _____ . Other students in the class are looking at the effects of watering, type of soil, and number of seeds planted in the same pot.

Name _____ Date _____

Directions: Read the questions. Choose the truest possible answer.

1. As your airplane lands in Florence, Italy, the pilot announces that the temperature on the ground is 8° C. What is the temperature in degrees Fahrenheit?

   Ⓐ -18° F
   Ⓑ 36° F
   Ⓒ 46° F
   Ⓓ 95° F

2. Your aunt Carmen has entrusted you with her hot chocolate recipe, which calls for 50 g of chocolate. If you want to make the drink, how many ounces of chocolate should you buy?

   Ⓕ 1 oz
   Ⓖ 2 oz
   Ⓗ 8 oz
   Ⓙ 20 oz

3. You are studying a small island in the Caribbean. The island has an area of 13 sq km. How big is it in square miles?

   Ⓐ 5 sq mi
   Ⓑ 8 sq mi
   Ⓒ 21 sq mi
   Ⓓ 34 sq mi

4. Your cousin Alain claims that he has gained 9 kg this year. How many pounds has he gained?

   Ⓕ 4 lbs
   Ⓖ 11 lbs
   Ⓗ 20 lbs
   Ⓙ 94 lbs

5. Your pet hamster weighed 120 g before she became pregnant and gained 80 g. How many kilograms does she weigh now?

   Ⓐ 0.12 kg
   Ⓑ 0.20 kg
   Ⓒ 1.2 kg
   Ⓓ 2.4 kg

6. If you and your brother share a bedroom 5 m wide and you want to paint your half of the room blue, how many centimeters should you measure to find the middle?

   Ⓕ 25 cm
   Ⓖ 50 cm
   Ⓗ 250 cm
   Ⓙ 5,000 cm

7. If gas in Namibia costs $1.30 per liter, how much does it cost per gallon?

   Ⓐ $2.00
   Ⓑ $3.00
   Ⓒ $5.00
   Ⓓ $9.00

8. Your grandparents' farm has 60 acres of pasture. They want to graze sheep on 1/3 of the pastureland. On how many hectares of pastureland do they plan to graze sheep?

   Ⓕ 8 ha
   Ⓖ 20 ha
   Ⓗ 86 ha
   Ⓙ 124 ha

STOP

Name_____ Date_____

Grade 8

Directions: Study the diagram. Label the parts of the microscope and write a brief description on the lines below.

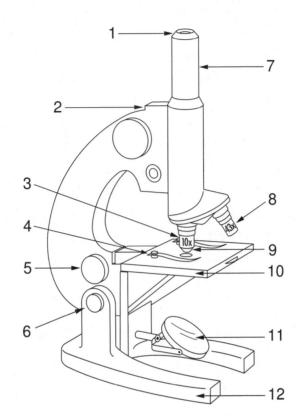

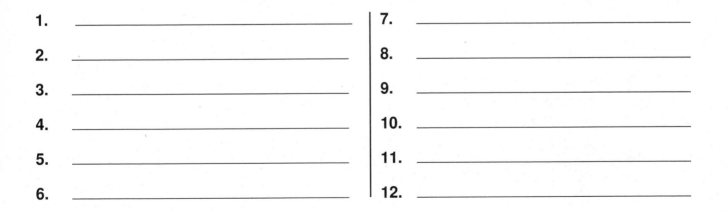

1. _____		7. _____	
2. _____		8. _____	
3. _____		9. _____	
4. _____		10. _____	
5. _____		11. _____	
6. _____		12. _____	

STOP

Grade 8

Directions: Read the text below. Use information from the text to help you answer questions 1–5.

Brian and Shavonta dissected a frog in science class. They removed the frog from a jar containing formaldehyde and placed it on the dissecting tray. Shavonta used a scalpel to make the first incision through the frog's lower abdomen. Next, Brian used scissors to cut up the midline of the frog, stopping at the chin. With the scalpel, Shavonta made a second incision horizontally across the width of the frog at the top of the vertical cut. Brian used the scissors to deepen the incision through the skin and muscle. Following their teacher's instructions, the students did not cut past the muscle layer. Then Shavonta used forceps to hold each flap of skin and muscle down while Brian pinned them on either side of the frog's body in the dissecting tray.

1. **Why was a scalpel the best tool for the first cuts?**
   - (A) Scalpels make quick, imprecise cuts.
   - (B) Scalpels can be sterilized.
   - (C) Scalpels are the sharpest tools used in classroom dissection.
   - (D) Scalpels are too dull to pose a safety hazard.

2. **Scissors are better to use than a scalpel when _____ .**
   - (F) cutting through soft tissue
   - (G) making a small, precise cut
   - (H) making a horizontal cut
   - (J) cutting through one layer only

3. **What would have happened if the students had cut past the muscle layer?**
   - (A) The frog would have bled.
   - (B) The frog's organs would have been sliced.
   - (C) They would have hit a fat layer in the chest.
   - (D) They would have lost the chance to examine the muscle.

4. **How are forceps used during dissection?**
   - (F) to extract organs
   - (G) to tear thin layers of tissue
   - (H) to move and hold specific parts of the organism being dissected
   - (J) to keep the organism from sliding around on the dissection tray

5. **Why did Shavonta and Brian pin the flaps to the sides of the frog?**
   - (A) to anchor the frog to the dissecting tray
   - (B) so they could see the frog's inner organs better
   - (C) because they were finished looking at the muscle layer
   - (D) to keep the formaldehyde from damaging the inner organs

Name_____ Date_____

Grade 8

Directions: Read the text below. Use information from the text to help you answer questions 1–5.

A science class is gathering information about a stream near their school using specialized, handheld data collection probes. They are looking at temperature, pH, and levels of dissolved oxygen, nitrates, and bacteria. The class collects data from the stream during second period science class on the first Monday of every month. Devon and Yuko have been assigned the spot farthest from the school building, near the Baileys' cow pasture. Other students collect data at different points along the stream. The students record data from the handheld probes and enter it into a computer program. Students at the school have been studying the stream for five years, and their teachers plan to continue with the study in the future.

1. **Why does collecting data every month provide more valuable information than collecting data once during the school year?**

    _____

    _____

2. **Why is it always good to collect data at the same time of day?**

    _____

    _____

3. **Ten years ago, Mr. Bailey planted many new trees along the stream. In the last five years, students and teachers have seen a decrease in nitrate levels. How could a computer program help them make a prediction about future nitrate levels?**

    _____

    _____

    _____

4. **Some of the students participating in the study are collecting data from a part of the stream that lies near an old coal mine. Pollution from a mine can cause water to be very acidic. If Devon and Yuko found a pH of 6, what pH might the students near the mine have found?**

    _____

    _____

5. **Fish breathe dissolved oxygen through their gills. Bacteria use oxygen as they work to break down dead plant matter. If a thunderstorm causes branches to fall in the stream near the school, what might happen to the fish population? Explain.**

    _____

    _____

    _____

0-7696-8068-2—*Science Test Practice*

Name_____ Date_____

Directions: Study the graph below. Use information from the graph to help you answer questions 1–4.

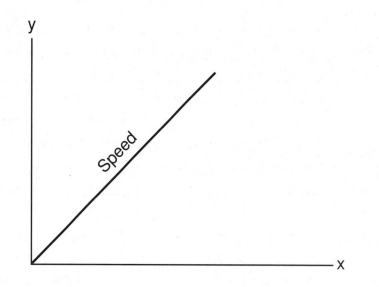

1. **Which label should be placed next to the x-axis?**

    (A) time

    (B) velocity

    (C) acceleration

    (D) temperature

2. **Which label should be placed next to the y-axis?**

    (F) direction

    (G) velocity

    (H) distance

    (J) temperature

3. **Which is the best title for this graph?**

    (A) Time it Takes to Heat a Substance

    (B) Acceleration of a Race Car

    (C) Location of an Object at Rest

    (D) Direction of a Pitcher's Throw

4. **What conclusion can you draw from this graph?**

    (F) Speed is a change in direction.

    (G) Speed is a change in acceleration.

    (H) Speed is a change in distance over time.

    (J) Speed is a change in temperature over time.

Directions: Study each table below. Use information from the tables to help you answer questions 1–6.

The table below shows the sizes of fox and rabbit populations on an island between 1999 and 2005.

Year	Fox Population	Rabbit Population
1999	79	785
2000	93	728
2001	112	690
2002	110	645
2003	91	668
2004	83	691
2005	76	739

1. How does the size of the fox population affect the size of the rabbit population from one year to the next?

_____

_____

2. Hunting season on rabbits opens once a year each summer. What is likely to happen to the fox population?

_____

_____

3. If a fox predator was introduced to this ecosystem, what would you expect to happen to the rabbit population? Explain.

_____

_____

This table shows the speed at which sound travels through air at different temperatures.

Temperature of Air (degrees Celsius)	Speed of Sound (meters per second)
100	354
80	347
60	340
40	334
20	327
0	321

4. Summarize the trend the table shows.

_____

_____

5. Why might this trend exist?

_____

_____

6. Carlos likes to clap his hands at the entrance to a canyon and listen for the echo's return. Describe changes he might notice in the echo over different seasons.

_____

_____

Grade 8

Directions: Study the graphs below. Use information from the graphs to help you answer questions 1–3.

In 2000, the school principal at Boyle High School launched a program to educate students on the benefits of a healthy diet.

This graph shows the average daily consumption of fresh juice at Boyle High School from 2002 to 2006.

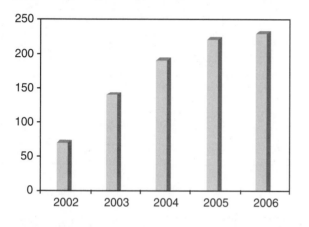

The graph below shows the average daily consumption of soda at Boyle High School from 2002 to 2006.

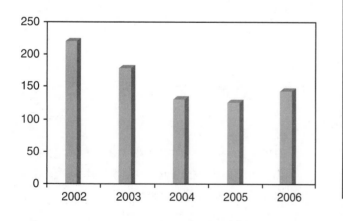

1. **What conclusion can you draw by looking at the graphs?**
   - (A) Students consumed the least soda in 2006.
   - (B) Students consistently prefer fresh juice to soda.
   - (C) Soda consumption has decreased steadily from 2002 to 2006.
   - (D) Fresh juice consumption has more than doubled since 2002.

2. **The second graph indicates that soda consumption changed the least from**
   - (F) 2002 to 2003.
   - (G) 2003 to 2004.
   - (H) 2004 to 2005.
   - (J) 2005 to 2006.

3. **In which year did Boyle High School students begin to consume more fresh juice than soda?**
   - (A) 2002
   - (B) 2003
   - (C) 2004
   - (D) 2005

Name_____ Date_____

Directions: Read the text below. Use information from the text to help you complete the activity. Use a separate sheet of paper if needed.

Stomach Ulcers

Ulcers are painful sores in the stomach. Before 1990, most doctors thought that ulcers were the result of too much acid in the stomach. People with ulcers were instructed to reduce stress in their lives and avoid coffee, alcohol, and other foods that cause the stomach to produce a lot of acid. However, many patients didn't get better.

In the course of his work, Australian scientist Robin Warren microscopically examined the stomach tissue of many ulcer patients. He noticed that about half their stomachs carried small curved bacteria he didn't recognize. The tissue near the bacteria was red and swollen. Interested, Dr. Warren and his colleague Barry Marshall took tissue samples from more patients. Once they knew what to look for, they realized that almost all the ulcer patients had the same bacteria. These bacteria represented a new species, later named Helicobacter pylori.

The medical community did not immediately accept the idea that ulcers were caused by bacteria. Scientists pointed out that the bacteria might invade after the ulcers developed. Dr. Marshall, who had no ulcers, decided to test his theory by infecting himself. He swallowed a culture of Helicobacter pylori. A few days later, he started to vomit. The vomiting continued for over a week. Examination showed that his stomach had developed the inflammation seen with ulcers.

Today, patients with ulcers are treated with antibiotics to kill the bacteria. With the use of antibiotics, more patients recover and live without stomach pain. In 2005, Dr. Warren and Dr. Marshall received the Nobel Prize in Physiology or Medicine.

1. **Below, provide detailed notes that summarize the scientists' experiment. Include the hypothesis and the results.**

    _____

    _____

    _____

    _____

    _____

    _____

Grade 8

Directions: Read the text below. Use information from the text to help you answer questions 1–3.

Human Population

Considering that human beings have lived on Earth for many thousands of years, it seems incredible that the most enormous increase in the human population has occurred only during the last 100 years.

Before the last century, the human population increased relatively slowly. On many occasions there were setbacks due to plagues, warfare, and natural disasters. The world's population didn't reach the 1 billion mark until about 1830. One hundred years later, however, the world's population suddenly stood at 2 billion. Then in 1975, less than fifty years later, it reached 3 billion.

In 1987, the world's population stood at an astonishing 5 billion, until just before the millennium when the total number of people living on Earth rose to over 6 billion. According to the World Health Organization, we are now growing at a rate of almost 77 million people each year.

1. **According to the information listed above, how would you describe the rate of population growth between the years 1930 to 1990?**

   (A) The population stayed the same.

   (B) The population actually decreased a little.

   (C) The population nearly doubled.

   (D) The population nearly tripled.

2. **What would be a reasonable explanation for the dramatic increase in human population during the past one hundred years?**

   (F) People no longer die in wars.

   (G) People have better health care, which extends their lifespan.

   (H) People no longer die from disease.

   (J) People have much larger families now than our ancestors ever did.

3. **The earth has limited space and resources. Scientists believe that the world's population is using resources at a rate that exceeds the planet's ability to support life. Discuss how you would plan to solve the problem of overpopulation.**

   _____

   _____

   _____

   _____

   _____

   _____

   _____

   _____

GO ON

Name_____ Date_____

Directions: Read the questions. Choose the truest possible answer.

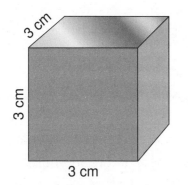

3 cm

3 cm

3 cm

1. **What is the volume of this cube?**
   - (A) 3 cm³
   - (B) 6 cm³
   - (C) 9 cm³
   - (D) 27 cm³

2. **Limonite, a common mineral found in metamorphic rocks, characteristically has 6 square sides. Each side is at a right angle to another adjacent side. Which geometric shape best describes the shape of limonite?**
   - (F) a square
   - (G) a rectangle
   - (H) a rectangular prism
   - (J) a cube

3. **A polygon shape could be found in which of the following natural features?**
   - (A) a whirlpool
   - (B) a mountain range
   - (C) a conch shell
   - (D) a human footprint

4. **Which of the following organisms has bilateral symmetry?**
   - (F) a dolphin
   - (G) a starfish
   - (H) a sponge
   - (J) a jellyfish

5. **Which of the following accurately describes the shape of the earth?**
   - (A) a circle
   - (B) a sphere
   - (C) an ellipse
   - (D) a parabola

6. **Which of the following best describes the paths of the planets in our solar system?**
   - (F) elliptical
   - (G) circular
   - (H) triangular
   - (J) horizontal

7. **Which phyla contain organisms with radial symmetry?**
   - (A) arthropods, annelids
   - (B) nematodes, chordates
   - (C) mollusks, echinoderms
   - (D) echinoderms, cnidarians

STOP

Name_____ Date_____

Directions: Read the text below. Use information from the text to help you answer the essay question. Use a separate sheet of paper if needed.

Hot Air Balloons

A hot air balloon is made up of 3 main parts:

The Envelope: The actual fabric balloon, which holds the air;

The Burner: The unit that propels the heat up inside the envelope;

The Basket: Where the passengers and pilot stand.

Propane gas is burned in order to heat up the air in the envelope. This is what enables the balloon to get off the ground and into the air. One of the pilot's jobs is to fire the burner on a regular basis during the flight to ensure that the balloon continues to fly. The heated air cannot leak from the hole at the bottom of the envelope.

When the pilot wants to move the balloon upward, he or she fires the burner, which shoots flames up into the balloon's envelope and heats the air inside it. To move the balloon downward the pilot pulls a long cord that runs down through the middle of the envelope to the basket. The cord opens the valve, letting hot air escape and decreasing the air temperature inside the envelope. When the pilot wants to move horizontally, the balloon needs to either ascend or descend. This enables the balloon to find different wind directions at different altitudes.

1. **Explain why a hot air balloon can fly through the atmosphere. Use information from the text and your own knowledge of science to illustrate which forces move a hot air balloon both vertically and horizontally.**

_____

_____

_____

_____

_____

_____

_____

━━━━━━━━━━━━━━━━━━━━━━━━━ **Grade 8** ━━━━━━━━━━━━━━━━━━━━━━━━━

Directions: Read the text below. Use information from the text to help you answer the essay question. Use a separate sheet of paper if needed.

Sunken Ships

After an especially busy week of classes, Mrs. Edwards ended Friday by showing a documentary on shipwrecks to her class. The documentary specifically focused on the area off the coast of North Carolina's Outer Banks known as the "Graveyard of the Atlantic." In this area of the Atlantic, more than 50 ships have sunk during the past three centuries. Scientists believe this is due to the topography of the shorelines and shallow shoals common to the region. The students were riveted by the story of Blackbeard the Pirate, whose ship, Queen Anne's Revenge, was sunk in the early 1700s.

After the class watched the documentary, Mrs. Edwards asked each student to perform an experiment at home using a plastic bowl, a metal bowl, a glass dish, and a bowl they made out of any material of their choosing. They were then to float each "ship" in a sink or tub full of water and record which ships floated. Then they were asked to simulate conditions that would cause each floating ship to sink. Each student was asked to bring the ships they made and the results of their experiments to class on Monday morning to discuss the results.

When the class met on Monday, Mrs. Edwards discovered that most of the students' bowls floated, even the ones they created themselves. The glass dish, however, did not.

"You all did very well," Mrs. Edwards congratulated them, "and I'm glad you had fun. Now I want you to write a paragraph explaining how our study of density and buoyancy last week relates to the experiments you did with your ships."

1. **Use your knowledge of buoyancy along with the information in the text to describe why some of the "ships" were able to float while others were not.**

_____

_____

_____

_____

_____

_____

Name_____ Date_____

==
Grade 8
==

Directions: Read the text below. Use information from the text to help you answer the essay question. Use a separate sheet of paper if needed.

Nuclear Power

As the end of the age of fossil fuels approaches, many countries are turning to nuclear energy as a source of power. Currently, three dozen countries use or plan to use nuclear reactors to generate power, but not all nations are taking part in this shift. Sweden has actually decided to phase out its use of nuclear power, and German leaders are debating whether Germany should gradually shut down its nuclear power plants.

Nuclear power uses a small amount of uranium or plutonium to produce a large amount of power, making it a more sustainable source of energy than fossil fuels. Surprisingly, nuclear reactors currently produce less radioactive waste than coal power plants, and they produce far less carbon dioxide. On the downside, nuclear reactors do produce radioactive waste, which poses a danger to humans and other living things.

Since nuclear power has both benefits and risks, the debate over its use continues. People who favor using nuclear power feel that it is relatively safe compared to traditional fuels and that future technology will improve its safety. Opponents feel the safety risks outweigh any economic benefits.

1.   **Your mayor has just announced that a nuclear reactor will be built in your town. Write a newspaper editorial in which you describe the benefits and risks of the use of nuclear power. Then explain whether you agree or disagree with the mayor's decision.**

_____

_____

_____

_____

_____

_____

_____

_____

0-7696-8068-2—*Science Test Practice*

Name_____ Date_____

Directions: Read the text below. Use information from the text to help you answer the essay question. Use a separate sheet of paper if needed.

Genetically Modified Organisms

While walking through a grocery store, you expect to see unblemished fruits and vegetables, foods with a long shelf life, and foods rich in nutrition. However, this is not always the case. Scientists hope that genetically engineered foods will help improve the quality of food in stores. Genetically engineered foods are created by manipulating the genetic composition of plants and animals. Scientists use the DNA of one organism to alter the DNA in another. As a result, food varieties are created that are resistant to pathogens and insects, produce higher yields, and have qualities desired by the food industry. Even with all these positive attributes of modified foods, the effects on human health of eating these foods are still not fully understood. Deciding whether the benefits outweigh the risks requires detailed studies of the new foods and their effects on humans and the environment.

1.   **Suppose that a government agency hires you to conduct research on genetically engineered foods. Using the information above, and your knowledge of science and technology, write an essay in which you discuss the following:**

    • two potential problems with genetically engineered foods;

    • two methods of maintaining consumer awareness about genetically engineered foods.

_____

_____

_____

_____

_____

_____

_____

_____

_____

_____

Name_____ Date_____

Directions: Read the questions. Choose the truest possible answer.

1. **The density of a substance determines its _____ .**
   - (A) texture
   - (B) buoyancy
   - (C) mass
   - (D) conductibility

2. **All of the following will sink in pure water *except* _____ .**
   - (F) lead
   - (G) mercury
   - (H) gold
   - (J) olive oil

3. **Which statement below is the correct explanation of how mountain-sized icebergs can float on the surface of the Arctic Ocean?**
   - (A) The Arctic Ocean's water contains less salt than the iceberg's water.
   - (B) The Arctic Ocean's cold temperature allows the iceberg to float.
   - (C) The density of the Arctic Ocean is higher than the density of the iceberg.
   - (D) The density of the iceberg is higher than the density of the Arctic Ocean.

Directions: Read the text below. Use information from the text to help you answer questions 4-5.

Leonard's grandfather has a sample of limonite, or "Fool's Gold," for Leonard's geology collection. Before he gives Leonard the sample though, his grandfather, a well-liked math professor, teases him with a question. "I happen to know," Leonard's grandfather tells him, "that this piece of "Fool's Gold" has a mass of 1,500 grams and a volume of 115 cm. If you want this for your collection, you must first tell me what the density of the sample is."

4. **Which of the following equations must Leonard use in order to answer his grandfather's question?**
   - (F) Density = mass + volume
   - (G) Density = volume • mass
   - (H) Density = $\dfrac{mass}{volume}$
   - (J) Density = $\dfrac{volume}{mass}$

5. **When Leonard uses the correct equation to find the density of the "Fool's Gold," his answer will be _____ .**
   - (A) 15.0 g/cm^2
   - (B) 11.5 g/cm^2
   - (C) 13.0 g/cm^2
   - (D) 30.0 g/cm^2

GO ON

Name_____ Date_____

Grade 8

Directions: Read the text below and fill in the blanks with words from the Word Bank.

Word Bank

solubility	liquid	molecules	solid
matter	dissolve	increases	

The Water Molecule

Astra's older brother Dov was helping her with her homework. "Let me begin by demonstrating the difference between a liquid and a solid," said Dov.

"My teacher told us that books are made of solid **1.** _____ ," said Astra.

"Yes, and so are marbles. They are made up of **2.** _____ that remain in fixed positions," explained Dov. He grabbed a bowl from his desk and filled it with water. Dov poured some marbles into the bowl. They made a clinking sound as they moved around in the water.

"Think of these marbles as molecules. I want to show you that, although the molecules in a **3.** _____ stay close together, they are free to move past one another," said Dov.

"So, a liquid does not always keep the same shape like a **4.** _____ does?" asked Astra.

"No, it does not. However, sometimes solids and liquids can be combined. Think about the time you tried to stir hot chocolate mix into ice water. Did the powder **5.** _____?" inquired Dov.

"No," replied Astra, "it just became clumpy."

"Right. You can see that hot chocolate powder, which is mostly sugar, does not dissolve in cold water," said Dov.

"Why?" asked Astra.

"The temperature of the water affects **6.** _____ . As the temperature increases, the solubility **7.** _____ .

"Now I understand what happened to my iced chocolate," laughed Astra.

 0-7696-8068-2—*Science Test Practice*

Grade 8

Directions: Read the questions. Choose the truest possible answer.

1. **The periodic table can be divided into three basic categories. Which of the following is _not_ one of the three major categories used on the periodic table?**

   Ⓐ metals

   Ⓑ alloys

   Ⓒ metalloids

   Ⓓ nonmetals

2. **Which of the following elements would you expect to best conduct heat and electricity?**

   Ⓕ hydrogen

   Ⓖ sodium

   Ⓗ copper

   Ⓙ carbon

3. **The elements helium, neon, krypton, and radon all belong to which of the following groups?**

   Ⓐ the nitrogen group

   Ⓑ the oxygen group

   Ⓒ the carbon group

   Ⓓ the noble gases group

4. **Which of the following substances is held together by physical rather than chemical means?**

   Ⓕ water

   Ⓖ soil

   Ⓗ oxygen

   Ⓙ gold

5. **What term would you use to describe a substance composed of two or more elements that are chemically combined?**

   Ⓐ an element

   Ⓑ a mixture

   Ⓒ a compound

   Ⓓ a solution

6. **How are saltwater and soil different?**

   Ⓕ Soil is a solution; saltwater is not.

   Ⓖ Soil is homogenous; saltwater is not.

   Ⓗ Soil is a compound; saltwater is not.

   Ⓙ Soil is a mixture; saltwater is not.

Name_____ Date_____

Directions: Read the text below. Use information from the text to help you complete the activity below. Use a separate sheet of paper if needed.

Up in Smoke

When the evening news shows images of large forest fires overtaking an open tract of natural land, we usually react with sorrow. The idea of flames burning out of control, destroying acres of vegetation, and forcing animals from their homes make most of us believe that immediately putting out the fire is the best solution. But conservationists have learned that fires often enrich a natural ecosystem. As a matter of fact, some species of coniferous trees cannot produce a seed unless their cones have been exposed to fire.

Large-scale experiments to determine the value of forest fires are often performed in national parks. Fires that are set by lightning strikes regularly burn in Yellowstone National Park. The fires often burn slowly for a while until the high winds associated with an approaching cold front fan the flames. When the fires are allowed to burn, they leave behind an uneven landscape with both heavily and lightly burned areas among untouched patches of land. In as little as two weeks after a fire, grasses and other herbaceous vegetation begin to grow. Within a year, there is abundant new growth in the burned areas. Within twenty-five years after a fire, the plant life in the park is very diverse. This proves that a landscape can recover from a seemingly devastating forest fire.

1. **Imagine you are a park ranger at Yellowstone National Park and a forest fire has just damaged a large section of the park. Write a report to your supervisor explaining possible causes, advantages, and disadvantages of the fire. Include a description of the land and a prediction of what the land might look like in ten years.**

_____

_____

_____

_____

_____

Grade 8

Directions: Read the text below and then complete the activities.

1. Examine the following substances and organize them into a table according to similar properties. Assign a symbol to the groups of substances with similar characteristics and use that symbol when you arrange your substances into the table. Place substances with the same symbol in the same column.

Substances		
cola	water	seltzer water
coffee	gasoline	maple syrup
motor oil	glass cleaner	bleach
shampoo	perfume	hair spray
cooking oil	egg whites	

2. Scientists arranged the elements in the periodic table into groups according to similar physical or chemical properties. Study group 17 or group 18 elements of the periodic table. Describe how the properties of the elements are similar.

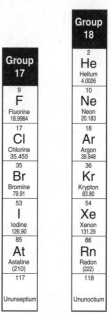

_____

_____

_____

_____

_____

_____

_____

_____

_____

Grade 8

Directions: Read the questions. Choose the truest possible answer.

1. **The atoms of any one specific element are always _____ .**
   - (A) ions
   - (B) alike
   - (C) arranged in pairs
   - (D) different

2. **A student has two boxes that are the same size. One is full of metal balls. The other is full of foam balls. Which of the following sentences is *true*?**
   - (F) The boxes have the same mass and volume.
   - (G) The boxes have the same mass, but different volumes.
   - (H) The boxes have the same volume, but different masses.
   - (J) The boxes have different masses and volumes.

3. **In which part of the water cycle does water enter the gaseous state?**
   - (A) in precipitation
   - (B) in condensation
   - (C) in evaporation
   - (D) in percolation

4. **The nucleus forms which part of an atom?**
   - (F) its outer shell
   - (G) its dense center
   - (H) its hollow center
   - (J) its energy cloud

5. **The number of protons found in the nucleus of an atom is referred to as the atom's _____ .**
   - (A) radioactive decay
   - (B) mass number
   - (C) half-life
   - (D) atomic number

6. **When scientists use radioactive decay to date the age of fossils, which element do they usually use?**
   - (F) oxygen
   - (G) iron
   - (H) carbon
   - (J) calcium

Name_____ Date_____

Grade 8

Directions: Read the text below. Use information from the text to help you answer questions 1–4.

On some backcountry trails in the mountains of Montana, a hiker might come across a sign with the warning, "Bears can run very fast." So just how fast can a bear run? On average, over a short distance, a bear can run approximately 30 miles per hour.

If you entered a grizzly bear in a race with the racehorse Smarty Jones, the record-breaking winner of a recent Kentucky Derby, and timed the two animals in a dead gallop to the first quarter-mile pole, the bear would win. A bear may not have the stamina of a thoroughbred racehorse during a race that lasts one mile, but in a quick burst of speed over a short distance, there is no contest.

1. **If a bear in Montana were running at full speed for thirty minutes, how far would it have traveled?**

    _____

2. **Based on the text, draw a line graph below that represents the approximate speed of the bear and the racehorse throughout the entire one-mile race.**

3. **According to the text, the bear's speed is 30 miles per hour. What additional piece of information would you need in order to determine the bear's velocity?**

    _____

    _____

4. **Describe why you presented the results that you did on your graph and how each result depicts the speed each animal can run over a certain distance.**

    _____

    _____

    _____

Name_____ Date_____

Grade 8

Directions: Read the text below. Use information from the text to help you answer questions 1–3.

Climbing Mount Everest

Stefan and his Sherpa guide Tung slowly climbed Mt. Everest by moving from camp to camp and resting during stops. The real challenge of their trek was dealing with the altitude gain and severe weather conditions rather than actual distance.

The distance between Base Camp and Camp One is 3.2 km. It took the two men 5 hours to walk from Base Camp to Camp One. After two days of rest, they spent another 5 hours traveling to Camp Two, which was 4.0 km away.

Climbing the next 4.0 kilometers to Camp Three took them 4 hours. The weather slowed them down tremendously, but they finally made it the 2.4 km to Camp Four in 8 hours.

After several more days of rest, the two made the final 2.4-kilometer ascent from Camp Four to the summit of Mt. Everest in 12 hours.

1. **What is the total distance the two men hiked between Base Camp and the summit of Mt. Everest?**
   - (A) 8.5 km
   - (B) 9.0 km
   - (C) 16 km
   - (D) 12 km

2. **If it took these two men twelve hours to travel 2.4 km from Camp Four to the summit of Mt. Everest, what was the average speed they were traveling?**

   _____

   _____

   _____

3. **Draw a graph showing the results of the entire climb.**

 0-7696-8068-2—*Science Test Practice*

Name_____ Date_____

Directions: Read the text below and fill in the blanks with words from the Word Bank.

═══════ **Word Bank** ═══════

trajectory	force	unbalanced	push	motion
projectile	accelerate	gravity	velocity	angle

The Cannon Shot

In 1776, near the little village of Paoli, Pennsylvania, occasional cannon shots broke the still air of cold November mornings. The thunderous cracks of the cannons marked the start of another day of small but bloody skirmishes between the American colonists and the British Redcoats in the fight for American independence. After each cannon was loaded with gunpowder and a cannonball was rolled down into its chute, the fuse was lit, firing the cannonball into the air. Once fired, the cannonball acted as a **1.** _____ moving through space on its **2.** _____ .

One of the reasons the cannonball serves as such a deadly weapon is because of the propelling **3.** _____ of the explosive in the cannon. This force provides the cannonball with a constant, or unchanging, horizontal **4.** _____ as it moves through the air. A force can be either a push or pull on an object. In the case of a cannonball that has just been fired into the air, the force is an explosive **5.** _____ .

As the cannonball sails through the air, it rises more and more slowly. But instead of dropping at a constant speed, the cannonball will **6.** _____ as it falls from the sky due to the force of **7.** _____ . According to Newton's Second Law of **8.** _____ , the forces that are acting on the cannonball are **9.** _____ forces.

Understanding how force acts upon a cannonball would help the soldiers predict where the cannonball would land. After missing a target, the soldiers would need to change the **10.** _____ of the cannon in order to place a more effective shot against the opposing army.

═══ Grade 8 ═══

Directions: Read each question. Write your answers on the lines provided.

1. What does energy measure?

   _____

   _____

   _____

2. What is the primary source of energy for plants?

   _____

   _____

   _____

3. How does the energy in a skateboard change as it rolls downhill?

   _____

   _____

   _____

4. At which point in the path of a pendulum is its potential energy highest?

   _____

   _____

   _____

5. Name four forms energy can take.

   _____

   _____

   _____

6. How do sound waves transmit energy?

   _____

   _____

   _____

7. How are light waves different from sound waves?

   _____

   _____

   _____

8. How are water molecules different in steam than in cool water?

   _____

   _____

   _____

9. What are units of heat called in the International System of Units?

   _____

   _____

   _____

10. How do molecules transfer energy to each other in a solid or liquid?

   _____

   _____

   _____

STOP

Directions: Read the text below. Use information from the text to help you answer questions 1–4.

Heat

When logs are burned in a wood stove, energy stored in the logs is released as heat. Burning is an exothermic reaction, or a chemical reaction that releases heat. A similar exothermic reaction occurs in a car engine. Inside the engine, air mixes with gasoline, and spark plugs release a spark that ignites the mixture. As the gasoline burns, heat is released, oxygen is consumed, and the gases in the engine expand dramatically. The engine uses the energy released by this reaction to power the car. Not all exothermic reactions are dramatic, though. For example, rust forms through a slow exothermic reaction in which iron combines with oxygen.

In exothermic reactions, the chemical bonds that are broken have higher energy than the chemical bonds that are formed during the reaction. Energy is released because it was not needed to form the new bonds. As a result, the products are more stable than the original reactants.

The reverse is true in an endothermic reaction. Endothermic reactions create products that are less stable and contain more energy than the reactants did. Instead of releasing energy, endothermic reactions absorb energy. These reactions require energy to occur. For instance, a cold pack is designed to cool your skin and muscles by taking in heat from its environment. Cold packs contain ammonium nitrate and water, held apart by a plastic divider. You activate the cold pack by breaking the divider. As the ammonium nitrate and water come into contact and react, they absorb heat.

1. **When hydrochloric acid reacts with sodium hydroxide, the products are sodium chloride (table salt) and water. Salt and water are more stable than hydrochloric acid and sodium hydroxide. Which type of reaction is this?**

   _____

2. **Heat must be added to food to cook it. Which type of reaction occurs in cooking?**

   _____

3. **A group of archaeologists have just entered the deepest part of an Egyptian tomb. After a short time, the flames of their torches begin to dwindle. What is the probably cause for this?**

   _____

4. **Amelie has a heat pack she uses to warm her hands in her coat pockets. To activate it, she squeezes the pack. Which type of reaction is occurring in the heat pack?**

   _____

Grade 8

Directions: Study the diagrams below. Use information from the diagrams to help you answer questions 1–8.

The top diagram shows light reflecting off a surface, while the lower diagram illustrates refraction of light through a medium.

Diagram 1

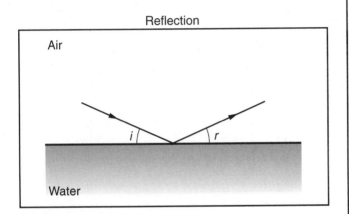

For reflection the the angle of incidence (i)=the angle of reflection (r).

Diagram 2

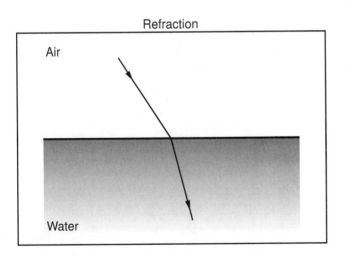

For refraction the light is bent when passing from one material to another, at an angle other than perpendicular.

1. In _____ , light bounces off a surface.

2. Mirrors work by _____ light.

3. Prisms act by _____ light.

4. Compared with the angle at which light hits a surface, the angle of reflection is _____ .

5. When you look at a straw in a glass of water by looking down into the glass, the straw appears to be bent. This happens because the light waves are _____ as they pass through the water.

6. Refraction occurs because as light waves pass from one medium (like air) into another medium (like water), they change _____ .

7. A prism separates light out into its component colors because each color has a different frequency and bends at a different _____ .

8. Black cars get hotter in the sun than white cars because they absorb more and _____ less light.

Directions: In the space below, draw a diagram of an electrical circuit made up of two light bulbs connected in series, two batteries, and an open light switch.

In a series circuit, the items drawing power (in this case, light bulbs) are connected to each other along the path of the electrical current, instead of being connected to the path separately as in a parallel circuit.

Grade 8

Directions: Read the passage below. Use information from the passage to help you answer questions 1–4.

Heat can be transferred by conduction, convection, or radiation. In conduction, atoms become hot because the atoms beside them are hot. The higher energy atoms move more rapidly. When the higher energy atoms collide with the lower energy atoms nearby, they transfer some of that energy to their neighbors. This action is similar to the way a cue ball hits another pool ball, and makes it move by transferring its energy. Conduction happens in solids, like the pot handle in the diagram below.

In convection, heated air or water transfers energy as it moves. Because hot water has more energy and faster moving atoms, it is less dense than colder water. The hot water rises to the top of the pot, but this distances the hot water from the heat source, so the water cools and sinks back to the bottom. These continual temperature changes cause currents to form in the pot. In boiling water, you can see the currents

Radiation is the transfer of energy through electromagnetic waves, which can occur in empty space. The light produced by an open fire is one form of electromagnetic radiation. Radiant energy emitted by the sun, which includes visible, infrared, and ultraviolet light, is called solar radiation.

1. **Instead of having one heating element at the bottom of the oven, some ovens cook food by circulating heated air. What is this process called?**
   - (A) convection
   - (B) conduction
   - (C) solar radiation
   - (D) electromagnetic radiation

2. **A photovoltaic cell on the roof of a solar-powered building converts solar energy to electricity. By which process does the sun transfer energy to the roof?**
   - (F) currents
   - (G) radiation
   - (H) convection
   - (J) conduction

3. **How is radiation different from conduction and convection?**
   - (A) Radiation produces currents.
   - (B) Radiation can occur in empty space.
   - (C) Radiation takes place only in the cores of stars.
   - (D) Radiation results from movement of high-energy atoms.

4. **Which of the following is an example of conduction?**
   - (F) a riptide in the ocean
   - (G) burning your hand on an oven rack
   - (H) cream sinking to the bottom of a cup of coffee
   - (J) your sunglasses blocking ultraviolet rays

STOP

Grade 8

Directions: Read the text below and study the diagram. Use information from both to help you answer questions 1–3.

Although amoebas live in pond water, they are not very common, so Mr. Harrison knew that sampling water near the school might not provide his science class with enough amoebas. Instead, he ordered a culture of amoebas for his students to look at under microscopes. Using an eyedropper, each team of students placed a drop of the culture on a microscope slide. Antoine and Ryla were sharing one microscope. Ryla placed a cover slip over the drop of water to flatten and protect it, then slid the microscope slide onto the stage and clipped it in place.

Antoine rotated the nosepiece so that the lens with the lowest magnification, 4x, was pointed at the slide. He turned on the light under the slide and looked through the eyepiece. The slide was a blur. Using the coarse adjustment knob, Antoine moved the lens in toward the stage, then moved it slowly back out again until the top of the cover slip came into focus. Then he switched to the lens with 10x magnification, and found the cover slip again. When Ryla took a turn focusing, she found an amoeba. She increased the magnification one more time, to 40x, and used the fine adjustment to focus on the amoeba. The amoeba Antoine and Ryla saw is diagrammed in the next column.

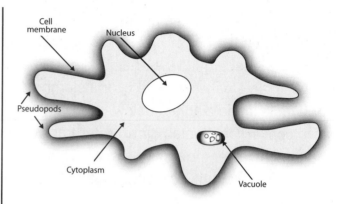

1. **Why did Antoine first focus on the cover slip?**

   _____

   _____

2. **When you are using a microscope, which magnification lens should you use first?**

   _____

3. **What structures are found in both a human cell and an amoeba?**

   _____

   _____

   0-7696-8068-2—*Science Test Practice*

Name_____   Date_____

Directions: Place the characteristics listed in the Word Bank in the appropriate section of the Venn diagram below.

─── **Word Bank** ───

Carry oxygen in blood	Take in nutrients	Excrete wastes	Capable of movement
Photosynthesize	Have specialized cells	Have cell walls	Move using flagella
Alive	Multi-cellular	Single-celled	

Characteristics shared by all three types of organisms should go in the space where all three circles overlap.

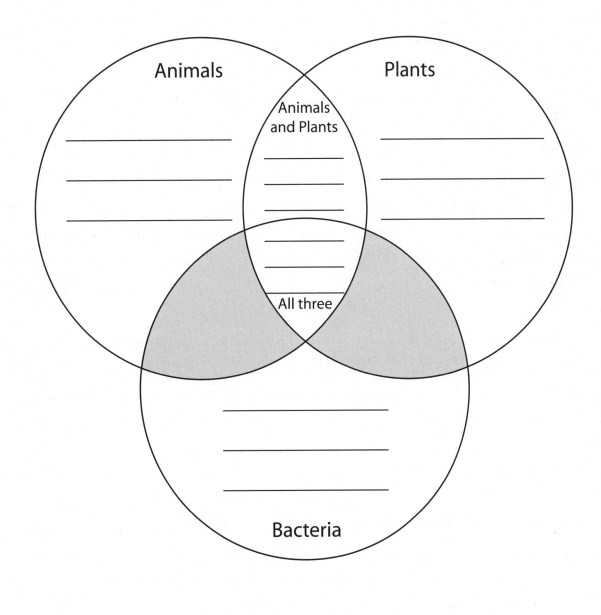

Name_____ Date_____

Directions: Read the following text and fill in the blanks with words from the Word Bank.

Word Bank

diversity	replicate	muscle	sexual reproduction	oxygen	water
sperm	mitochondria	identical	two	division	mitosis
calcium	single-celled	reproduce	chromosomes	carbon dioxide	46
1–2	sexually	nucleus			

To function properly, the cells in the human body need a steady supply of oxygen,

1. _____ , inorganic chemicals, and organic compounds. In every cell, 2. _____

use 3. _____ and nutrients to produce energy. Water, which makes up nearly 70% of the

body's tissues, is used to deliver oxygen to cells, and remove 4. _____ .

Some tissues need specific minerals to function. For instance, bone formation requires

phosphorus, magnesium, fluorine, and 5. _____ . Potassium and sodium are required for

6. _____ and nerve function.

Each cell has a natural lifespan. Red blood cells, for instance, live for about four months. When a

cell dies, it is generally replaced by a new cell. New cells are produced through cell 7. _____ .

8. _____ organisms, such as bacteria, 9. _____ by splitting in half. Each cell

10. _____ produces two identical cells. Although the process is more complicated in

humans, reproduction of most cells in the human body also results in two cells identical to the parent

cell. The information needed to exactly 11. _____ each human cell is contained in the

cell's DNA, which is grouped into 12. _____ in the cell's 13. _____ .

Nearly all human cells have 14. _____ chromosomes. When a skin cell divides, it

produces 15. _____ copies of each chromosome, and one copy goes to each daughter

cell. Each daughter cell is 16. _____ to the parent skin cell. Skin cells divide more

frequently than most human cells. The top layer of a person's skin is replaced 17. _____

times a month!

Unlike bacteria, humans reproduce 18. _____ . Unlike all other human cells, egg and

19. _____ cells contain 23 chromosomes. During fertilization, these chromosomes join to

produce a zygote with 46 chromosomes. Because half of a baby's chromosomes come from his

father and half from his mother, the baby is not identical to either parent. 20. _____

introduces 21. _____ into the human population. Every person has a new combination

of characteristics and abilities.

STOP

Name_____ Date_____

Directions: Read the following text and fill in the blanks with words from the Word Bank.

Word Bank

neurons	heart	white	clots	skeletal	connective
smooth	red	electrical	energy	squamous	cuboidal
columnar	brain	absorb			

Human beings are not only made up of many different cells, but of many different kinds of cells. Muscle cells, epithelial cells, connective tissue cells, blood cells, and nerve cells all look different and perform different functions.

Muscle cells contract and relax in response to nerve impulses, causing movement. The human body has three types of muscle cells. **1.** _____ muscle cells control movement of bones, such as our arms and legs. Cardiac muscle cells control contraction of the **2.** _____ . The esophagus, stomach, and intestines, which contract to digest food and move it along the digestive tract, are made up of **3.** _____ muscle.

Humans also have three types of epithelial cells: squamous, cuboidal, and columnar. Skin is made up of **4.** _____ cells. **5.** _____ epithelial cells line body cavities and glands, while **6.** _____ epithelial cells line the stomach and intestines. Epithelial cells protect the underlying tissue. The epithelial cells lining the stomach and intestines also **7.** _____ nutrients from food.

Bone, blood, cartilage, and fat are all types of **8.** _____ tissue. These tissues support and protect organs as well as hold them together. Bone supports the body, cartilage cushions joints, and fat cushions and insulates organs. Fat also stores **9.** _____ . Blood supports tissues by transporting oxygen and nutrients throughout the body.

Blood contains several different types of cells. Oxygen is carried by **10.** _____ blood cells. **11.** _____ blood cells protect the body from infection. Platelets help to heal wounds by forming **12.** _____ .

Nerve cells, or **13.** _____ , are found in the **14.** _____ , spinal cord, and peripheral nervous system. They transmit **15.** _____ impulses and release neurotransmitters that affect our movements, thoughts, and feelings.

Grade 8

Directions: Read the questions. Choose the truest possible answer.

1. **Bodies have four basic levels of organization. Which is the correct order, from smallest to largest?**
   - (A) cell, tissue, organ, system
   - (B) tissue, system, organ, cell
   - (C) cell, organ, system, organism
   - (D) tissue, organism, organ, system

2. **In which organ are blood cells made?**
   - (F) bone
   - (G) heart
   - (H) liver
   - (J) skin

3. **How do skeletal muscles allow the body to move?**
   - (A) They contract and pull on bones.
   - (B) They relax and push on bones.
   - (C) They connect to nerves, which contract.
   - (D) They push on nerves, which relax.

4. **What does your heart do?**
   - (F) It exchanges oxygen for carbon dioxide.
   - (G) It gets rid of extra blood volume.
   - (H) It replaces old platelets and blood cells.
   - (J) It pushes blood through your vessels.

5. **Which of these is *not* a function of the stomach?**
   - (A) absorbing nutrients from food
   - (B) digesting food with muscles
   - (C) killing bacteria
   - (D) digesting food with enzymes

6. **What does a healthy large intestine do?**
   - (F) It completes the digestion of food.
   - (G) It removes extra fluid from the body.
   - (H) It absorbs water and excretes solid waste material.
   - (J) It filters waste material from the blood.

7. **In which organ does a human fetus normally develop?**
   - (A) fallopian tube
   - (B) ovary
   - (C) uterus
   - (D) scrotum

8. **Which organ helps control blood sugar level?**
   - (F) pancreas
   - (G) gall bladder
   - (H) stomach
   - (J) tongue

STOP

Grade 8

Directions: Read the questions. Choose the truest possible answer.

1. **Which of the following fights against infection and disease by attacking antigens that enter the body?**
   - Ⓐ capillaries
   - Ⓑ red blood cells
   - Ⓒ platelets
   - Ⓓ white blood cells

2. **Diabetes is an example of a chronic disease. Which of the following is the best explanation of a chronic disease?**
   - Ⓕ a disease that lasts for only a short amount of time
   - Ⓖ a disease that can be transmitted from person to person
   - Ⓗ a disease that can be controlled, but not cured
   - Ⓙ a disease that is caused by bacteria or other microorganisms

3. **A person is most likely to become infected with HIV from _____ .**
   - Ⓐ infected blood
   - Ⓑ infected mucus
   - Ⓒ sweaty skin
   - Ⓓ a doctor's needle

4. **Which of the following statements about antibiotics is true?**
   - Ⓕ Antibiotics become more powerful against infection with frequent use.
   - Ⓖ Antibiotics do little to prevent the spread of infectious diseases.
   - Ⓗ Antibiotics are the best defense against a cold.
   - Ⓙ Antibiotics can cure bacterial infections, but not viruses.

5. **Which of these diseases is least likely to be a result of tobacco use?**
   - Ⓐ lung cancer
   - Ⓑ emphysema
   - Ⓒ heart disease
   - Ⓓ diabetes

6. **Which of the following is true about sickle cell anemia?**
   - Ⓕ It is transmitted by mosquito bites.
   - Ⓖ It is inherited.
   - Ⓗ It is from a virus that is common in cities.
   - Ⓙ It is a bacterial infection.

7. **Which body system is attacked in a person infected with AIDS?**
   - Ⓐ the circulatory system
   - Ⓑ the immune system
   - Ⓒ the reproductive system
   - Ⓓ the respiratory system

Name_____ Date_____

Grade 8

Directions: Read the text below. Use information from the text to help you answer questions 1–5.

Plant Reproduction

Rather than eating food, plants make their own food through photosynthesis. Photosynthesis is the process by which plants convert carbon dioxide, water, and energy from the sun's light into sugars.

Photosynthesis takes place in two stages. During the first stage, plants capture light energy from the sun. Chlorophyll, the chemical that makes plants green, absorbs light energy for photosynthesis. The second stage of photosynthesis is where the plant uses the captured energy to produce sugar. The plant uses carbon dioxide and water and converts these products into glucose. Oxygen and a small amount of water are produced as waste products during this stage.

Photosynthesis is basically the opposite of cellular respiration, the process by which animals transform energy. Mitochondria in animal cells take in oxygen and glucose and convert them into carbon dioxide and water in a process that releases energy the cells can use.

In the ocean, algae and plants such as sea grass produce their food through photosynthesis. These plants live close enough to the ocean's surface to capture light energy from the sun. In the ocean depths, where light does not penetrate, plants cannot grow. However, some bacteria live in deep-sea vents more than a mile below the ocean floor. They produce energy from carbon dioxide and other chemicals, such as hydrogen and sulfur, in a process called chemosynthesis. Organisms like these may have been the first forms of life on Earth.

1. **How is photosynthesis related to cellular respiration?**

   _____

   _____

2. **What is the initial source of most of the energy in an ocean ecosystem?**

   _____

3. **What are the waste products of photosynthesis?**

   _____

4. **What two things do animal cells convert into energy during cellular respiration?**

   _____

5. **How do bacteria living in deep-sea vents get the energy they need to live?**

   _____

   _____

   _____

 0-7696-8068-2—*Science Test Practice*

Grade 8

Directions: Read the following text and fill in the blanks with words from the Word Bank. Not all words will be used.

Word Bank
---

n	gamete	egg	2n	sperm	zygote
female	male	fertilization	23	46	chromosomes
meiosis	cells				

In the human life cycle, **1.** _____ takes place to produce an offspring. The

2. _____ provides the **3.** _____ and male provides the **4.** _____ .

Both of these cells are referred to as **5.** _____ cells and are represented by the

symbol **6.** _____ . The single cells fuse to form a **7.** _____ . These

8. _____ are represented by the symbol **9.** _____ . The fertilized cell has

10. _____ chromosomes and has been through the process of **11.** _____ .

The cell division process of **12.** _____ occurs when the **13.** _____ number

is reduced.

Directions: Read each question. Write your answers on the lines provided.

14. What are some things adults can do to slow down the effects of aging?

_____

_____

_____

15. Why is it difficult to know when adulthood begins? Explain.

_____

_____

_____

Grade 8

Directions: Read the questions. Choose the truest possible answer.

1. Which organ of the digestive system is responsible for most nutrient absorption?

    (A) stomach
    (B) esophagus
    (C) large intestine
    (D) small intestine

2. In the lungs, oxygen is exchanged for _____ .

    (F) water
    (G) glucose
    (H) nitrogen oxide
    (J) carbon dioxide

3. About what percentage of the human body is made up of water?

    (A) 10%
    (B) 30%
    (C) 50%
    (D) 70%

4. Which organs remove waste from the blood and control blood volume?

    (F) lungs
    (G) tonsils
    (H) arteries
    (J) kidneys

5. What is the main function of sweat?

    (A) cooling the body
    (B) eliminating waste
    (C) hydrating the skin
    (D) eliminating excess water

6. When glucose levels in the blood are too high, the pancreas secretes _____ .

    (F) bile
    (G) insulin
    (H) calcium
    (J) adrenaline

7. Which of the following bodily conditions is controlled by a positive feedback mechanism?

    (A) blood clotting
    (B) blood pressure
    (C) body temperature
    (D) glucagon production

8. How many major bones does the adult human body have?

    (F) 59
    (G) 118
    (H) 206
    (J) 310

Name_____ Date_____

Grade 8

Directions: Study the diagram below. Use information from the diagram to help you answer questions 1–6.

Purple flowers are dominant. This Punnett square shows the crossing of a purple-flowered pea plant with a white-flowered pea plant.

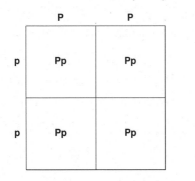

	P	P
p	Pp	Pp
p	Pp	Pp

P = purple-flower allele   p = white-flower allele

1. **How many of the four pea plants have purple flowers?**

   _____

2. **Which plants in the Punnett square are homozygous for flower color? Which are heterozygous?**

   _____

   _____

3. **One of the offspring of this generation (genotype Pp) transferred its pollen to another flower of the same generation (also of genotype Pp). Fill in the Punnett square below to describe this cross.**

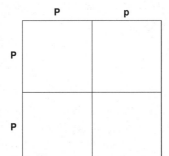

	P	p
P		
P		

4. **How many of the four pea plants resulting from this cross have purple flowers?**

   _____

   _____

5. **How many of these four plants are heterozygous for flower color?**

   _____

   _____

   _____

6. **If you crossed a purple-flowered pea plant of unknown genotype with a white-flowered plant, and half of the plants resulting from the cross had white flowers, what could you deduce to be the genotype of the purple-flowered plant? Explain.**

   _____

   _____

   _____

   _____

0-7696-8068-2—*Science Test Practice*

Directions: Read the text below and study the diagram. Use information from both to help you answer questions 1-2.

Cystic fibrosis, a serious lung disease, is inherited in an autosomal recessive manner. A person with one cystic fibrosis gene (Ff) is a carrier but is not affected by the disease. The following Punnett square shows the children of two carriers.

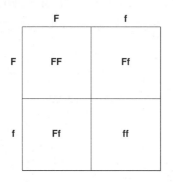

1. **What percentage of the couple's children are likely to be carriers of cystic fibrosis but be unaffected by the disease?**

   _____

2. **What percentage of the couple's children are likely to have cystic fibrosis?**

   _____

Directions: Read the text below and study the diagram. Use information from both to help you answer questions 3-4.

Huntington's disease, a degenerative disease of the nervous system that does not cause symptoms until adulthood, is inherited in an autosomal dominant manner. A person with one gene for Huntington's disease (Hh) will have the disease. The following Punnett square shows the children of one person with Huntington's disease and one person who does not carry the disease.

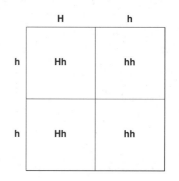

3. **The famous folksinger Woody Guthrie died of Huntington's disease. His son Arlo does not have Huntington's. Since his mother did not have the disease, how likely was Arlo Guthrie to have it?**

   _____

4. **Most fatal diseases are not inherited in a dominant manner. Why is Huntington's disease an exception to this rule?**

   _____

   _____

   _____

Grade 8

Directions: Read each question. Write your answers on the lines provided.

1. Male white-crowned sparrows sing a characteristic song to claim territory and attract females. In the normal course of events, all male white-crowned sparrows sing the same type of song. However, if a sparrow is raised with no other sparrows around him, his song will be very different. Is the sparrow's song learned or inherited? Explain.

   _____

   _____

2. Some orchids have flowers resembling female wasps, and male wasps try to mate with them. When the wasps move from plant to plant, they carry pollen the plants need for fertilization. However, the wasps can tell that the flowers do not act like female wasps. After repeated exposure to the flowers, the male wasps stop approaching them. Based on the information above, identify a learned trait, an inherited trait, and a trait that could be either inherited or learned.

   _____

   _____

   _____

3. A well-known way of testing a dog's intelligence is to cover it with a large towel and see how long it takes for the dog to find its way out. Researchers have done this with many dogs and found that the time the dog needs to find its way out is related to its breed. For example, border collies find their way out very quickly, while basset hounds usually take a long time. Is the speed at which a dog gets out of a towel a learned trait or an inherited trait? Explain your answer.

   _____

   _____

   _____

4. Why are adopted children of particular interest in determining whether human traits are learned or inherited?

   _____

   _____

Grade 8

Directions: Read the text below. Use information from the text to help you answer questions 1–3.

State Park Ecosystem Exploration

Ms. Daymond's science class took a field trip to Eno River State Park to practice identifying plants. The parkland is a forest on the East Coast. Although the land along the river has been farmed and logged in the past, thirty years ago a conservation association converted it into a state park.

When a farmed field in this part of the country is abandoned, the first plants that take over the land are grasses. Then pines sprout and rapidly grow tall. Hardwood trees like oaks grow up under the pines, but because the pines block the sun they do not reach their full height until the pines begin to die, perhaps a century after they sprouted.

As they approached the riverbank, Paco watched a huge bird soar above the treeline. He called to the teacher and pointed. It was a great blue heron, with a wingspan of nearly six feet. The class also found some ducks swimming in a shady part of the river. Ms. Daymond explained that the ducks eat plants and seeds, whereas the great blue heron uses its long, sharp beak to spear fish and frogs.

Jamila noticed some ragged tree stumps and asked Ms. Daymond what could have cut the trees down. Ms. Daymond suggested that it was the work of beavers, which are common in the park. She told the students the beavers eat plants in addition to the bark of certain trees.

1. **Grasses are the first plants to grow in an abandoned farm field in this part of the country. Why didn't the students see many grasses on their field trip?**
   - (A) People walking in the state park have killed the grass.
   - (B) Rhododendrons are poisonous to grass.
   - (C) The ducks eat plants and seeds and have eaten too much of the grass.
   - (D) Grass doesn't grow well in the shade of the new trees.

2. **The sun, water, and soil in the park are _____ .**
   - (F) abiotic factors
   - (G) examples of biodiversity
   - (H) proof of succession
   - (J) biogeochemical cycles

3. **If the fish population increased, what would most likely happen to the great blue heron population?**
   - (A) It would relocate.
   - (B) It would increase.
   - (C) It would decrease.
   - (D) It would stay the same.

Name_____   Date_____

Directions: Read the text below. Use information from the text to help you answer questions 1–3.

Producers, Consumers, and Decomposers

Organisms that make their own food instead of eating other organisms are called producers. Trees, grass, and other plants are all examples of producers. These organisms produce energy through photosynthesis. Not all producers obtain their energy from the sun. Certain bacteria produce energy through a process called chemosynthesis. Producers are the source of all the food in an ecosystem.

Producers are eaten by consumers, which are organisms that eat other organisms for energy. All animals are consumers. Consumers are classified into three groups according to what they eat. Field mice, cattle, and cottontail rabbits are known as herbivores because they eat only plants. Carnivores, such as wolves, spiders, and frogs, eat only other animals. Black bears, chickens, and other organisms that eat both plants and animals are known as omnivores.

When organisms die, they are then broken down by decomposers. After the organisms are broken down, the raw material is returned to the environment. For instance, some bacteria get their energy by digesting the tissues of dead plants or animals. Without decomposers, the bodies of plants and animals would pile up until they covered all the earth!

1. **You sometimes see mushrooms growing on logs because they get energy from dead plant matter. Are mushrooms producers, consumers, or decomposers?**

   _____

   _____

2. **All animals are consumers, but they are divided into first-level (or primary), second-level (or secondary), and third-level (or tertiary) consumers. In some areas, there are even fourth-level consumers. Consider an ecosystem where beetles eat plants, frogs eat beetles, snakes eat frogs, and hawks eat snakes. What level consumer is a snake?**

   _____

3. **In the African grassland, giraffes, zebras, and impalas eat grasses, shrubs, and trees. As these animals graze, they must keep watch for predators, such as lions and cheetahs. Name the consumers and producers in this ecosystem. Classify the consumers as herbivores, omnivores, or carnivores.**

   _____

   _____

   _____

   _____

   _____

Name_____ Date_____

Directions: The Word Bank contains the names of animals that live in the Sonoran desert ecosystem. Read the words in the Word Bank, and then answer the questions.

```
┌──────────────────── Word Bank ────────────────────┐
│  rat          coyote        prickly pear cactus    pocket mouse │
│  hawk         rattlesnake                          │
└────────────────────────────────────────────────────┘
```

1. **Draw a food web that includes all the organisms listed in the Word Bank.**

2. **Which organisms in this ecosystem are producers?**

   _____

3. **Which organisms are consumers?**

   _____

Grade 8

Directions: Read the text below. Use information from the text to help you answer questions 1–3.

A Garden Ecosystem

At dawn, tree swallows living above a hilltop garden leave their nests in search of food. The swallows hunt for cabbage butterflies that sail through trellised pea vines. Upon sighting the birds, the white insects try to hide in the shade of the leaves and dangling pods.

On the ground below the birds, a large black rat snake weaves through the damp grass to find a sunny spot. She heads toward the wooden teepees that support the sugar peas. From her perch on the teepee, the snake watches the swallows glide back to their nesting boxes, their beaks full of insects for their hungry chicks. Basking in the hot sun has stirred the snake's appetite. She is ready to find food.

The swallows spot the snake's long black form approaching the trellis. The threat of danger causes the swallows to react. They begin to circle and dive to warn other organisms of the snake's presence. In another part of the garden, meadow voles scurry around the red drumhead cabbage in search of plentiful caterpillars.

The snake is patient. In time, sensing no danger, the birds continue their own hunt. The voles, also intent on finding food, move quickly among the plants. The sun is hot and the air on the soil's surface is becoming steamy, even in the shade. The snake lies still, waiting.

1. **Describe how the activities of the organisms in the garden ecosystem might change if the temperature starts to drop quickly.**

   _____

   _____

   _____

   _____

2. **Pick one organism in the garden and explain its dependence on an abiotic (or non-living) feature of its garden ecosystem.**

   _____

   _____

3. **Identify the predators in this garden ecosystem and describe what might happen to the plants growing in this garden if one or more of the predators are removed.**

   _____

   _____ STOP

Directions: Read the questions. Choose the truest possible answer.

1. **Which organisms in the ocean would you expect to have the smallest population?**
   - (A) whales
   - (B) phytoplankton
   - (C) conch shells
   - (D) tuna

2. **What is similar about an organism that dies in a deciduous forest and an organism that dies in the ocean?**
   - (F) They both become part of the soil.
   - (G) They both help to create coral reefs.
   - (H) They both add nutrients to their environment.
   - (J) They both become phytoplankton.

3. **The size of most of the producers in the ocean environment can be described as _____ .**
   - (A) larger than most trees
   - (B) about the size of a grain of sand
   - (C) the same size as consumers living in the ocean
   - (D) microscopic

Directions: Read each question. Write your answers on the lines provided.

4. **If the producers of an ocean environment were removed, what would you expect to happen to the other organisms in the ecosystem? Explain.**

   _____

   _____

   _____

   _____

   _____

5. **Describe the importance of sunlight to the ocean environment. Explain how aquatic producers and consumers use sunlight.**

   _____

   _____

   _____

   _____

   _____

   _____

Name_____ Date_____

Directions: Read the questions. Write your answers on the lines provided.

1. Compare and contrast antigens and pathogens and give one example of each.

   _____

   _____

   _____

2. What are antibodies and what is their relationship to antigens?

   _____

   _____

   _____

3. Explain how fevers start, and how they actually help you stay healthy.

   _____

   _____

   _____

4. Describe two ways that harmful pathogens can be passed to and among humans.

   _____

   _____

   _____

Name_____ Date_____

Directions: Read the text below. Use information from the text to help you answer the essay question. Use a separate sheet of paper if needed.

Your Body's Repair Shop

People who drive have a responsibility to keep their car in good condition. They must regularly visit an auto repair shop to keep their vehicles working on the inside and outside. Otherwise, their car could experience problems, break down, or simply stop running altogether. The human body is no different. In order to live a productive and enjoyable life, people have a responsibility to maintain their bodies. Imagine living a healthy lifestyle as your daily trip to the auto repair shop, where you make sure everything is running smoothly.

How can you live a healthy lifestyle? First of all, make time for exercise. Exercise, especially aerobic exercise that increases the heart and distributes more oxygen throughout the body, is crucial to good health. Its short term benefits are obvious, but the long term effects are even more important. The more often you exercise, the stronger your heart, lungs, and bones become. Exercise also burns calories and generates more energy for everyday activities. When you play sports for healthy reasons, everybody wins!

Also important to your health is the practice of good hygiene. You may have some control over making your body stronger, but you don't have any control over external elements that may affect you. To stay healthy, you have to always stay on the alert against disease and infection. The single best way to prevent the spread of sickness is to wash your hands regularly. Also, basic body maintenance should include bathing, washing your hair, brushing and flossing your teeth, and always applying sunscreen on sunny days.

1. **Using information from the passage and your knowledge of science, explain which healthy habit described above you think is most important and why.**

_____

_____

_____

_____

_____

_____

Grade 8

Directions: Read each question. Write your answers on the lines provided.

Directions: Read the questions. Choose the truest possible answer.

1. **A 16-year-old boy and his 11-year-old sister are spending the day at the park. He is playing basketball and she is reading a book. Which person should eat to obtain more calories, and why?**

_____

_____

_____

_____

2. **What is the different between complete proteins and incomplete proteins? Give an example of a food that has each.**

_____

_____

_____

_____

3. **Vitamin C is very important because it** _____ .

   (A) helps fights disease

   (B) builds strong bones

   (C) protects red blood cells

   (D) assists with blood clotting

4. **What is the only vitamin that your body can make?**

   (F) Vitamin A

   (G) Vitamin B

   (H) Vitamin C

   (J) Vitamin D

5. **What are the six classes of nutrients?**

   (A) fruits, grains, meat and beans, milk, oils, and vegetables

   (B) amino acids, calories, carbon, cholesterol, fats, and fiber

   (C) carbohydrates, proteins, fats, water, vitamins, and minerals

   (D) calcium, chloride, magnesium, phosphorus, potassium, and sodium

6. **What information is not found on a typical Nutrition Label?**

   (F) Serving information

   (G) Malnutrition warning

   (H) Percentage of daily values

   (J) Number of calories per serving

Grade 8

Directions: Read the questions. Choose the truest possible answer.

1. Both the arctic fox and snowshoe hare are examples of mammals with a coat that changes color during the year. In winter their coat is white, and in summer it turns to various shades of brown. Which of the following best explains this particular adaptation?

    (A) They change color in response to the severe arctic temperatures.

    (B) They change color to allow them to blend in with their surroundings.

    (C) They change color as they grow older.

    (D) They change color depending on the amount of food they have eaten.

2. Which is not an adaptation that helps a polar bear survive the Arctic's sub-freezing temperatures?

    (F) black skin

    (G) clear, hollow hairs

    (H) enormous layer of fat

    (J) large canine teeth

3. How is an elephant seal similar to a polar bear?

    (A) both can move quickly

    (B) both hibernate during the coldest months

    (C) both possess thick layers of blubber under their skin

    (D) both are omnivores

4. Reptiles use the environment to keep their body temperatures within a healthful range. Which behavior is typical of a reptile that needs to increase its body temperature?

    (F) hiding under a rock

    (G) digging into sunny sand

    (H) lying full-length on a sunny rock

    (J) floating in water

5. Some birds spend nearly their entire lives flying over or floating on the ocean. This kind of bird has the ability to excrete salt from an opening on its face. What does this adaptation allow the bird to do?

    (A) drink ocean water

    (B) float above the water

    (C) fly very fast

    (D) blend in with white rocks

6. In extreme summer heat, most people use air conditioning to cool off. People also have other ways of dealing with heat. When the body gets very hot, it has natural ways of cooling down. Explain how the body can cool itself down naturally.

    _____

    _____

    _____

    _____

STOP

Directions: Read the questions. Choose the truest possible answer.

1. **The bull moose with the largest antlers almost always wins the right to breed with any cow moose in his territory. Based on this knowledge, which sense is the cow moose most likely to use in order to pick her mate?**

   (A) smell
   (B) hearing
   (C) taste
   (D) sight

2. **What would not be a factor in the growth of a bull moose's antlers?**

   (F) his age
   (G) his inherited genes
   (H) an abundant food supply
   (J) the air temperature

3. **Crocodiles are carnivores that spend part of their time in the water and part of their time on land. Alligators are not closely related to crocodiles, but look almost identical. What is the most likely explanation for their similarity?**

   (A) They both come from the same area.
   (B) Their body shapes and parts are common in many animals.
   (C) They help each other by looking alike but acting different.
   (D) They fill similar niches in different areas.

4. **An alligator's tail is very strong, as well as long and covered with hard, sharp scales. Which behavior does this adaptation *not* allow the alligator to do?**

   (F) swim fast
   (G) knock animals over
   (H) move quickly on land
   (J) rotate under water

5. **What is hibernation? What causes it? What might vary the length of time that an animal hibernates?**

   _____
   _____
   _____
   _____
   _____
   _____
   _____
   _____
   _____
   _____

Name_____ Date_____

Directions: Read the text below. Use information from the text to help you answer questions 1–4.

The Saguaro

In the deserts of the American West, some plants have found ways to adapt to obstacles such as intense sun and extremely dry conditions. Many plants, like the saguaro cactus, have developed unusual methods of coping.

The saguaro has a shallow root system. However, like many other cactus species, the saguaro is a succulent plant. Although the tall saguaro has a straight trunk that is hard and waxy to the touch, the inside of the plant is wet and porous. Surrounding the woody skeleton is water-holding tissue and a thick skin that prevents water loss.

Like most species of cactus, the saguaro does not have leaves. Instead, it has sharp spines extending out from the trunks and side branches. Most animals find it difficult to chew on the cactus because of the spines.

Without some of these adaptations, the saguaro and other cactus plants would not be able to survive in the extreme environment of the desert.

1. **A cactus is often called a succulent plant, which means that it can _____ .**
   - Ⓐ withstand intense heat
   - Ⓑ hold a great deal of moisture
   - Ⓒ only live in the desert
   - Ⓓ survive very cold temperatures

2. **Which of these would *not* help a saguaro survive in the desert?**
   - Ⓕ sharp spines
   - Ⓖ thick skin
   - Ⓗ wet, porous insides
   - Ⓙ green appearance

3. **The saguaro is prone to being broken down by storm-force gusts of wind. This is *most likely* because of _____ .**
   - Ⓐ its shallow root system
   - Ⓑ its lack of leaves
   - Ⓒ its tall, straight trunk
   - Ⓓ its porous insides

4. **Some types of desert cactus seem to jump out and grab on to passersby. Then parts of the cactus break off. How might this help the cactus?**
   - Ⓕ It is a warning to animals that they'll get hurt if they try to eat it.
   - Ⓖ The cactus gains nutrients from the blood of the animals it attaches to.
   - Ⓗ The broken parts get dispersed to different areas and new cacti grow there.
   - Ⓙ It prevents the cactus from growing too large and becoming prone to wind damage.

Grade 8

Directions: Read the text below. Use information from the text to help you answer questions 1–4.

Extinct Species

One of the most famous extinct species is the dodo. Dodos were flightless birds that lived only on the island of Mauritius. In the 1600s, people came to the island in ships. The sailors cut down the forests that the dodos lived in. The animals that came with the sailors destroyed the dodo nests. Some of the dodos were hunted and eaten. After about 80 years, the species was extinct.

Perhaps the most shocking story of extinction is that of the passenger pigeon. When the first Europeans arrived in North America, the species numbered in the billions. By the mid-19th century, however, large-scale commercial hunting caused a drastic drop in its numbers. During some years, over a million birds were shipped to east coast cities as a cheap source of meat. The birds were also hunted for sport, with hundreds of thousands used in shooting practice. By the early 1900s, the passenger pigeon was extinct.

Species that seem to be in danger of becoming extinct today are called endangered species. Many governments throughout the world have laws and programs to try to protect them.

1. **Which of the following statements is true?**
   - (A) All extinctions are caused by people.
   - (B) It is not possible to predict extinctions.
   - (C) People are trying to prevent some extinctions.
   - (D) Most extinctions are caused by natural disasters.

2. **The dodos died out because _____ .**
   - (F) they overpopulated their island and used up their resources
   - (G) people destroyed their habitat and hunted them
   - (H) they couldn't fly
   - (J) a meteorite hit their island

3. **Which of the following best explains the relationship between extinction and biodiversity?**
   - (A) As extinctions increase, biodiversity increases.
   - (B) As extinctions increase, biodiversity decreases.
   - (C) As biodiversity increases, extinction decreases.
   - (D) As biodiversity decreases, extinctions decrease.

4. **Which of these actions is unlikely to protect endangered species?**
   - (F) setting limits on hunting of endangered animals
   - (G) adopting an acre of rain forest
   - (H) logging and clear-cutting forests where endangered animals live
   - (J) captive breeding of endangered animals

STOP

Grade 8

Directions: The trilobite began as an organism swimming in the ocean. The diagrams below illustrate the fossilization of a trilobite. For questions 1–3, briefly explain the process shown in each stage.

Death

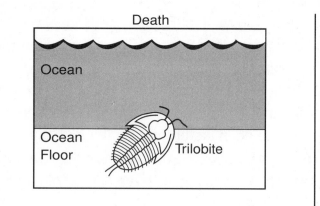

1. _____

_____

Deposition

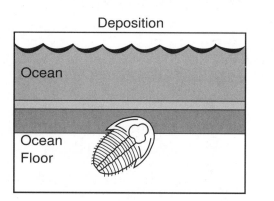

2. _____

_____

Permineralization

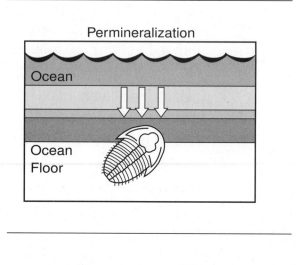

3. _____

_____

Directions: Read the questions. Choose the truest possible answer.

4. **Which natural disaster would *most likely* be associated with the formation of a fossil?**

    Ⓐ a forest fire

    Ⓑ a hurricane

    Ⓒ a landslide

    Ⓓ a blizzard

5. **How might a paleontologist determine the age of a fossil?**

    Ⓕ by counting its rings

    Ⓖ by determining the age of the soil layer in which it was found

    Ⓗ by burning a portion of the fossil

    Ⓙ by placing a drop of acid on the fossil

6. **Under normal conditions, which organism is most likely to be fossilized?**

    Ⓐ an animal made only of cartilage

    Ⓑ a daffodil flower

    Ⓒ a butterfly

    Ⓓ any animal with a shell or bones

7. **What can we learn from fossils?**

    Ⓕ how specific types of rock are formed

    Ⓖ why extinct species died out

    Ⓗ the history of every living organism

    Ⓙ where the ancient oceans were

Name_____   Date_____

Grade 8

Directions: The diagram below shows a cross section of Earth's layers. Complete the diagram by filling in the blanks.

Note: This diagram is not drawn to scale.

Layers of the Earth

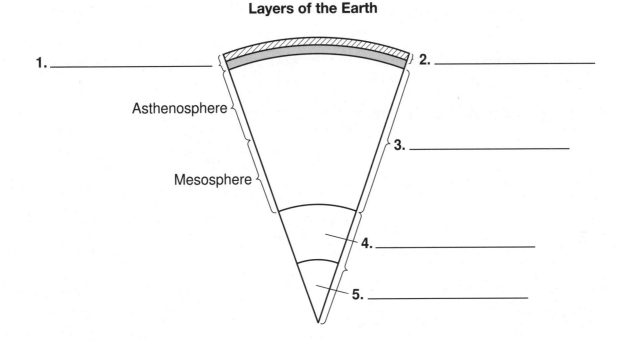

1. _____   2. _____

Asthenosphere }

3. _____

Mesosphere }

4. _____

5. _____

Directions: Read the questions. Choose the truest possible answer.

6. **Earthquake waves can travel from Earth's surface to the center of Earth. About how many kilometers do they travel?**
   - (A) 60 km
   - (B) 600 km
   - (C) 6,000 km
   - (D) 60,000 km

7. **Which of the following *best* describes the physical properties of Earth's mantle?**
   - (F) solid
   - (G) liquid
   - (H) solid but has the ability to flow
   - (J) liquid but is unable to flow

8. **The inner core of Earth remains solid because of extreme _____ .**
   - (A) heat
   - (B) mass
   - (C) motion
   - (D) pressure

STOP

     0-7696-8068-2—*Science Test Practice*

Directions: Read each question. Write your answer on the lines provided.

1. **What is the theory of plate tectonics?**

   _____

   _____

   _____

2. **What is Pangaea, and how is it related to continental drift?**

   _____

   _____

   _____

3. **Name the three ways that plates interact with each other at their edges.**

   _____

   _____

   _____

4. **Name two ways that mountains are formed at convergent plate boundaries.**

   _____

   _____

   _____

5. **What kind of boundary exists where two tectonic plates meet in California, and what is the effect of their movement there?**

   _____

   _____

   _____

   _____

Name _____ Date _____

Directions: Study the illustration below. Use words from the Word Bank to label 1–6.

Directions: Read each question. Write your answers on the lines provided.

─── **Word Bank** ───

crater	vent	side vent
lava flow	pipe	magma chamber

Volcanic Eruption

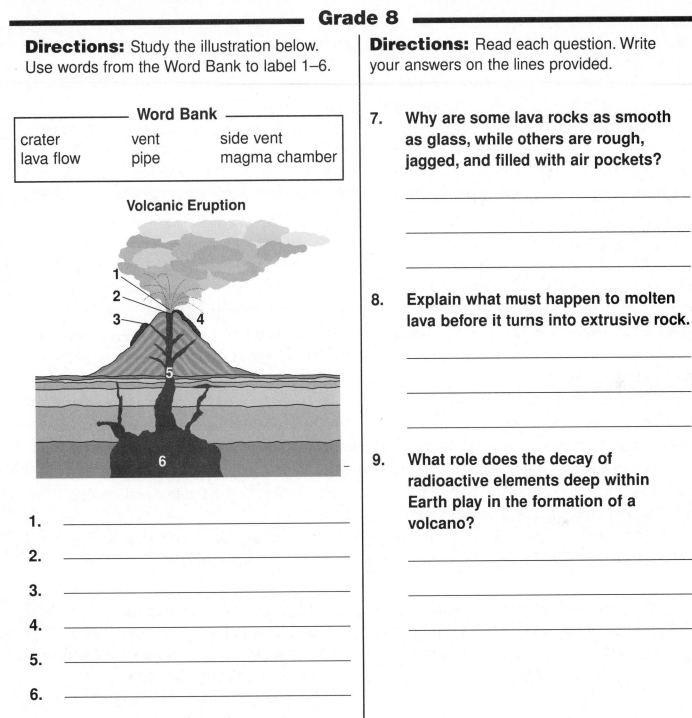

1. _____

2. _____

3. _____

4. _____

5. _____

6. _____

7. **Why are some lava rocks as smooth as glass, while others are rough, jagged, and filled with air pockets?**

_____

_____

_____

8. **Explain what must happen to molten lava before it turns into extrusive rock.**

_____

_____

_____

9. **What role does the decay of radioactive elements deep within Earth play in the formation of a volcano?**

_____

_____

_____

Directions: Read the passage below. Use information from the passage to help you answer questions 1–2.

Natural Destructive Forces

It's hard to imagine, but the oak forests that blanket much of the northeastern United States grow out of soil that was once bare rock. If not for the interaction between the animals, plants, and weather over many, many years, the forests would never have come to be.

Many things must happen before an oak forest can exist. Picture a large, flat rock before you. Right now it is only a rock, but think of the changes that will take place when the top layer of this rock is exposed to the environment.

At this point the bare rock has few places for seeds to stay and germinate. Even if they do, this flat rocky surface won't hold any water. Before a plant seed can grow here, the rock must change. Rain, snow, ice, sun, and wind all help generate those changes. Once the weather changes the surface of the rock, tiny species of lichen can get a foothold. Soon moss grows and sends its thin, rootlike parts down into cracks in the once solid rock. Those cracks now allow more water to seep in.

The water and the roots help make the cracks even larger, allowing bigger plants to drop their seeds there and grow. Animals are then attracted to the plants. As the animals walk over the surface of the rock to visit the plants, small particles of rock break down even more. As more plants grow and die on the rock's surface and more animals frequent the area, the once solid rock turns into deeper soil. The soil is composed of the remains of dead plants and animals, minerals from the bedrock, and air pockets that hold moisture.

Over a very long time, the rock surface is replaced by rich soil that easily fosters wildflowers, shrubs, and tall trees like oaks. It is now a forest that started as a bare rock.

1. **Occasionally, you can see a pine tree that looks like it is growing right out of a rock. What must be true about the rock in this situation?**

_____

_____

_____

2. **It is common to see lichens on boulders in forests, especially on slopes. In which two parts of the rock-to-forest progression do you see lichens and oak trees? Why can they be seen together?**

_____

_____

_____

_____

_____

_____

Name_____   Date_____

Grade 8

Directions: Complete the diagram of a rock cycle below using words from the Word Bank.

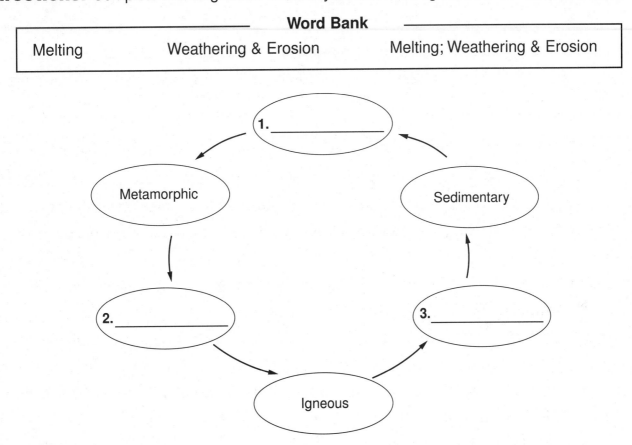

Directions: Read each question. Write your answers on the lines provided.

4. **In which type of rock formation would you expect to find a dinosaur fossil and why?**

_____

_____

5. **Give one example of weathering and erosion that has a positive effect where it occurs and one example that has a negative effect where it occurs.**

_____

_____

6. **Briefly describe how heating and cooling play a role in the transformation of metamorphic rock into igneous rock.**

_____

_____

Name_____ Date_____

Directions: Read the text below and fill in the blanks with words from the Word Bank.

Word Bank

leafy	loam	organic	habitat	bedrock	proportion
topsoil	profile	weathering	food chains		

Where would you be without soil? Almost every green plant on Earth is dependent on soil in order to grow. Those green plants provide the start of most of our **1.** _____ . Good soil is necessary to grow our food crops on farms. Our forests need soil. Grass prairies need soil. Marshes, wetlands, and swamps all require soil. Even a desert ecosystem is dependent on its soil.

If you were to create a recipe for soil, you would need the following ingredients: rocks, minerals, the wastes and remains of plants and animals, water, and air. The plant and animal remains are also known as **2.** _____ material. Some soils have a lot of minerals and some have more plant and animal matter. The make-up of the soil will help determine what kind of **3.** _____ is found there. Soil types are also affected by rainfall, wind, and rubbing, also known as **4.** _____ .

Soils are identified by their five horizons in the **5.** _____ . The O horizon is the soil's surface, or **6.** _____ layer. This is the place where plant and animal matter decompose. The A horizon is called the **7.** _____ . The B Horizon is where the subsoil is found. And finally, the C Horizon is known as the **8.** _____ . This is a site of mostly weathered parent material (meaning partly broken-down minerals).

The mineral portions of the soil are made up mostly of sand, silt, and clay. The soil texture refers to the **9.** _____ of each type of particle. A combination of sand, silt, clay, and humus would be called **10.** _____ .

Grade 8

Directions: Fill in the three missing phases of the water cycle in the blank lines on the diagram shown below.

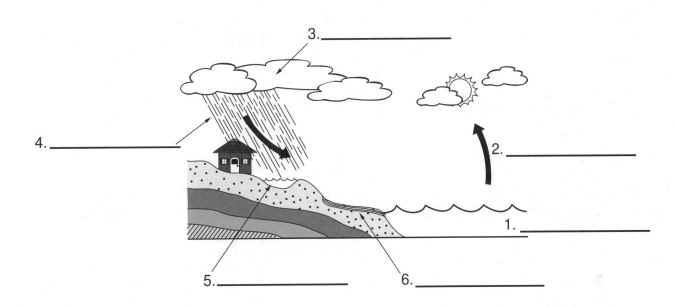

3._____

4._____

2._____

1._____

5._____

6._____

Directions: Read each question. Write your answer in paragraph form on the lines provided.

7. **Describe the journey of a water molecule as it moves from a liquid to a gas to a solid, giving specific examples.**

_____

_____

_____

_____

8. **What are some problems associated with surface water runoff, and what can be done to reduce these problems?**

_____

_____

_____

_____

_____

Name_____ Date_____

Grade 8

Directions: Read the questions. Choose the truest possible answer.

1. **At which layer of the atmosphere would you expect a passenger jet to fly?**
   - Ⓐ the troposphere
   - Ⓑ the stratosphere
   - Ⓒ the mesosphere
   - Ⓓ the thermosphere

2. **When water vapor condenses within the troposphere, what natural feature is formed?**
   - Ⓕ the aurora borealis
   - Ⓖ tornadoes
   - Ⓗ lightning
   - Ⓙ clouds

3. **Ozone is naturally found in the stratosphere. What does this ozone layer protect us from?**
   - Ⓐ chlorofluorocarbons
   - Ⓑ ultraviolet light
   - Ⓒ gaseous water molecules
   - Ⓓ carbon monoxide

4. **Which atmospheric level has the coldest temperatures?**
   - Ⓕ the thermosphere
   - Ⓖ the mesosphere
   - Ⓗ the stratosphere
   - Ⓙ the troposphere

5. **Which gas, added to Earth's atmosphere by green plants, makes life more suitable for animals?**
   - Ⓐ nitrogen
   - Ⓑ hydrogen
   - Ⓒ carbon dioxide
   - Ⓓ oxygen

6. **Earth's atmosphere is mostly composed of which substances?**
   - Ⓕ metals
   - Ⓖ gases
   - Ⓗ liquid water molecules
   - Ⓙ condensed water molecules

7. **What would you expect to happen to the air temperatures if you could rise up through all the levels of the atmosphere?**
   - Ⓐ They would constantly decline.
   - Ⓑ They would constantly increase.
   - Ⓒ They would rise and then fall.
   - Ⓓ They would remain the same.

 0-7696-8068-2—*Science Test Practice*

Name_____ Date_____

Directions: Read the text below. Use information from the text to help you answer questions 1–3.

Clouds and Climate

Clouds help us predict the weather. Actually, current weather conditions determine the various shapes, heights, and colors of clouds, but those same cloud shapes, heights, and colors give us a hint of the weather to come.

There is always water vapor in the air. When the air temperature has cooled to its point of saturation (or dew point), the water molecules in the air form clouds. Forces that move the air around in the atmosphere determine the shape and size of clouds. Approaching cold fronts cause clouds to rise high into the sky, while clouds forming in warm air stay closer to the ground.

There are as many as eight major cloud types. Some are more familiar to us than others. The clouds you usually associate with gray, rainy days are stratus clouds. Cumulus clouds look like large cotton balls in the sky on sunny days. They often appear low to the ground and then disappear within 15 minutes of forming. However, some cumulus clouds may develop into giant cumulonimbus clouds, also known as thunderheads. These clouds often form when the air close to the ground is warm and moist, and a cold front is approaching. Their huge, flat tops sometimes contain large amounts of ice that may fall to the ground as rain or hail once the thunderstorm begins.

1. **Why are thunderstorms more common in the summer than in the winter?**

    _____

    _____

2. **Why is the climate east of the Rocky Mountains drier than the climate west of them?**

    _____

    _____

    _____

3. **Bar Harbor, on the coast of Maine, seldom gets very hot. The town is known for its crisp, clear summer weather, and for its summer days of dense fog. Explain how it is possible that these different weather conditions are both common in Bar Harbor.**

    _____

    _____

    _____

STOP

Grade 8

Directions: Read the text below. Use information from the text to help you answer questions 1–2.

Ocean Currents and Climate

It may be hard to believe, but currents in the ocean have a big effect on our climate. Ocean currents are one of the factors that regulate temperature on the earth. Each current follows a particular path as it moves water from one area to another. For example, the Gulf Stream is a surface current in the Atlantic Ocean that moves warm water from the Equator to colder areas in the North. This has a warming effect on northern climates. In a similar way, cool water moves in surface currents from the poles to the Equator, causing cooler weather than would otherwise occur.

Ocean surface currents are produced primarily by wind blowing over the oceans. The currents move in the same general directions that the winds blow. The earth's rotation affects these directions. It causes winds and currents flowing from the Equator toward the poles to curve to the East, and winds and currents flowing from the poles toward the Equator to curve to the West. These deflections of winds and currents are evidence for the Coriolis Effect, which also causes hurricanes to rotate.

Deep ocean currents can also affect an area's climate. Deep currents are caused by density differences. The cold, salty water at the poles is very dense compared to the water around it. Thus, cold, salty, dense water sinks toward the bottom of the ocean and flows toward the Equator. Surface currents can cause shallow water to move away from an area. Then, the cold, deep water can upwell, or rise toward the surface. When the cold water reaches the surface, it can absorb heat from the atmosphere, producing cooler climates.

1. **How do deep currents affect climate?**

_____

_____

_____

2. **What do you think would happen to the earth's climate if surface currents suddenly disappeared?**

_____

_____

_____

Name_____   Date_____

━━━━━━━━━━━━━━━ **Grade 8** ━━━━━━━━━━━━━━━

Directions: Complete the concept map below.

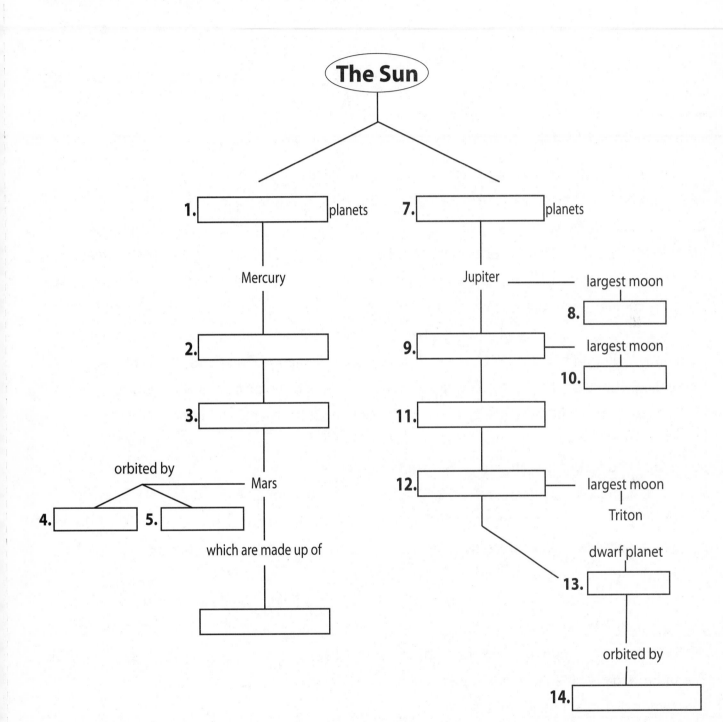

Name_____ Date_____

Grade 8

Directions: Read the following passage and fill in the blanks with words from the Word Bank.

Word Bank

x-ray's	stars	month	2 million	winds	permanent
maximum	magnetic	ejection	quickly	prominences	rotation
hydrogen	solar activity	helium	coronal	radiation	aurora
convection	11 years	photosphere	dark	chromosphere	solar flares

The sun is only one of many **1.** _____ , but it is the center of our solar system and a vital source of energy for Earth. A huge ball of gas, the sun produces energy when **2.** _____ fuses into **3.** _____ at its core. This energy travels out from the core, through the **4.** _____ zone and into the **5.** _____ zone, a layer of swirling gases. Then it passes through the three layers of the sun's atmosphere. In the **6.** _____, nearest the core, temperatures are approximately 6,000 K. Two thousand kilometers above this layer begins the **7.** _____, which extends for another 8,000 km before transitioning into the corona. The corona stretches over a million kilometers into space. Temperatures in the corona reach **8.** _____ K. Charged particles escaping the corona form solar **9.** _____.

Sunspots were first recorded by Galileo, who could see them through his telescope. Compared with the areas around them, sunspots are **10.** _____. The sun displays more sunspots in some years than others. Sunspot prevalence varies over the **11.** _____ cycle, with maximums approximately every **12.** _____. Although sunspots are not **13.** _____, their movements have been used to track the sun's **14.** _____. Being more fluid than Earth, the sun spins more **15.** _____ at its equator than at its poles. One rotation of the sun takes approximately one Earth **16.** _____.

Sunspots are associated with intense **17.** _____ fields. These forces may cause the arching blasts of gas known as **18.** _____, which shoot material into space at speeds up to 1,000 km/s. The bright and violent eruptions called **19.** _____ also start near sunspots. These eruptions and solar winds transmit ultraviolet light and **20.** _____ to Earth, sometimes disrupting radio signals.

During a sunspot **21.** _____, the sun may appear to have a halo. This is called a **22.** _____ mass **23.** _____, or CME. CMEs set up electrical currents around Earth that **24.** _____ gases in the atmosphere. Close to the poles, these currents cause the multicolored lights of the **25.** _____.

Grade 8

Directions: Read the questions. Choose the truest possible answer.

1. **A constellation that is circumpolar _____ .**

   Ⓐ is visible all year long

   Ⓑ cannot be seen from Earth

   Ⓒ is based on similar star patterns

   Ⓓ contains the brightest stars

2. **Why could sailors steer by Polaris?**

   Ⓕ It stays in the same place and remains visible throughout the year.

   Ⓖ It is an unusually bright star.

   Ⓗ It is the closest star to Earth.

   Ⓙ It moves north and follows a predictable pattern throughout the year.

3. **Approximately how many stars are in the Milky Way?**

   Ⓐ 30,000

   Ⓑ 1 trillion

   Ⓒ 2 million

   Ⓓ 15 billion

4. **What shape is the Milky Way galaxy?**

   Ⓕ spiral

   Ⓖ circular

   Ⓗ elliptical

   Ⓙ irregular

5. **Where is the sun located within the Milky Way?**

   Ⓐ on one arm

   Ⓑ on the center

   Ⓒ at the northernmost point

   Ⓓ at the southernmost point

6. **How did Edwin Hubble realize the universe was expanding?**

   Ⓕ Planets were becoming less dense.

   Ⓖ It was becoming more difficult to view the planets.

   Ⓗ Stars in other galaxies were moving away from Earth.

   Ⓙ Black holes were becoming more common.

7. **The color of a star indicates its _____ .**

   Ⓐ location

   Ⓑ size

   Ⓒ age

   Ⓓ temperature

STOP

Name_____ Date_____

Grade 8

Directions: Read the questions. Choose the truest possible answer.

1. **Which planets travel fastest?**
   - (A) large planets
   - (B) small planets
   - (C) planets farthest from the sun
   - (D) planets closest to the sun

2. **Which planetary object takes longest to move around the sun?**
   - (F) Earth
   - (G) Pluto
   - (H) Mercury
   - (J) Saturn

3. **What do we call the period of time that Earth takes to orbit the sun?**
   - (A) day
   - (B) year
   - (C) week
   - (D) month

4. **Which force causes planetary objects to revolve around the sun?**
   - (F) gravity
   - (G) friction
   - (H) magnetism
   - (J) tropism

Directions: Complete the diagram of phases of the moon.

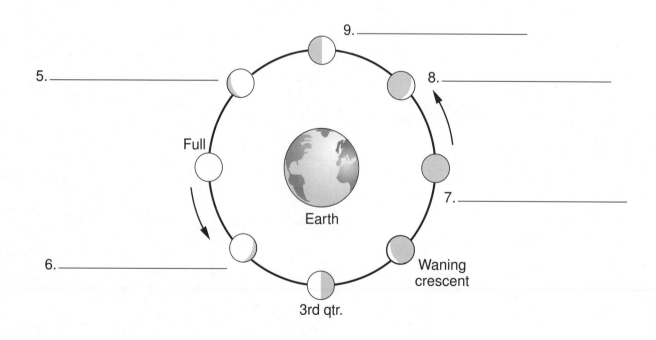

9. _____

5. _____

8. _____

Full

7. _____

Earth

Waning crescent

6. _____

3rd qtr.

STOP

Name_____ Date_____

Grade 8

Directions: Read the questions. Choose the truest possible answer.

1. If your weight on Earth is 490 N, what is your mass?
   - (A) 20 kg
   - (B) 30 kg
   - (C) 50 kg
   - (D) 70 kg

2. What is the acceleration due to gravity on Earth?
   - (F) 1.6 m/s^2
   - (G) 5.3 m/s^2
   - (H) 7.2 m/s^2
   - (J) 9.8 m/s^2

3. If your mass is 70 kg, what is your weight on Earth?
   - (A) 7 N
   - (B) 13 N
   - (C) 371 N
   - (D) 686 N

4. Gravity on the surface of the moon is only 16% as strong as gravity on Earth's surface. If your weight on Earth were 400 N, what would your weight be on the moon?
   - (F) 25 N
   - (G) 64 N
   - (H) 400 N
   - (J) 6400 N

5. On Mars, the acceleration due to gravity is 3.7 m/s^2. If your mass were 50 kg, what would your weight be on Mars?
   - (A) 14 N
   - (B) 50 N
   - (C) 73 N
   - (D) 185 N

6. If you were in outer space with an elephant and the elephant charged you, could you stop her?
   - (F) Yes, because you would both be weightless.
   - (G) Yes, because your mass would be the same as hers.
   - (H) No, because her weight would still be more than yours.
   - (J) No, because her inertia would be the same as on Earth.

7. Where could you jump highest while exerting the same amount of force?
   - (A) on Mars
   - (B) on Earth
   - (C) on the sun
   - (D) on the moon

STOP

Name_____   Date_____

Directions: Read the questions. Choose the truest possible answer.

1. **Which of these statements is an example of a good hypothesis?**
   - (A) The tennis ball rolled 10 meters in 5.8 seconds.
   - (B) Copper conducts heat twice as fast as tungsten.
   - (C) Did the ancient Egyptians know how to produce electricity?
   - (D) The king cobra is the most terrifying snake on Earth.

2. **Which of the following is an example of a good scientific observation?**
   - (F) The elephant's leg felt like the bark of a tree.
   - (G) The bacteria looked unhealthy when bleach was added to the solution.
   - (H) The watermelon is 0.5 meters long and weighs 10 kilograms.
   - (J) The baseball will travel 80 meters in 2 seconds.

3. **What is usually the last step of the scientific method?**
   - (A) to make observations
   - (B) to collect data
   - (C) to test a hypothesis
   - (D) to draw conclusions

4. **Which of the following has no place in a scientific statement?**
   - (F) a belief
   - (G) a theory
   - (H) a law
   - (J) a hypothesis

5. **The one factor that you change in a scientific experiment is referred to as the _____ .**
   - (A) constant
   - (B) control
   - (C) independent variable
   - (D) dependent variable

6. **Which of the following is not a kind of scientific classification?**
   - (F) the Mohs Scale of Hardness
   - (G) plant taxonomy
   - (H) carnivorous animals
   - (J) solar flares

7. **Electrons in an atom _____ .**
   - (A) are stationary, and cover the surface of the nucleus
   - (B) are stationary, and are all the same distance from the nucleus
   - (C) travel around the nucleus in one specific path, forming rings
   - (D) travel around the nucleus in an unpredictable path, forming a cloud

GO ON

Grade 8 Posttest

8. **What is the half-life of a sample of radioactive material?**

   (F) the average number of particles ejected by the material per year

   (G) the approximate number of people exposed to the material per year

   (H) the amount of time it takes for half of the sample to decay

   (J) the amount of time a person can be safely exposed to the sample

9. **Which of the following is true regarding enzymes and catalysts?**

   (A) A catalyst is a type of enzyme.

   (B) An enzyme is a type of catalyst.

   (C) A catalyst is usually changed by the reaction it is involved in.

   (D) A catalyst is always shown in chemical equations it is involved in.

10. **The way a mineral reflects light is its _____ .**

    (F) streak

    (G) luster

    (H) specific gravity

    (J) cleavage

11. **One element changes into another during radioactive decay, which is known as the process of _____ .**

    (A) photosynthesis

    (B) respiration

    (C) transmutation

    (D) osmosis

12. **The rate of decay of a nucleus is measured by its _____ .**

    (F) circumference

    (G) diameter

    (H) half-life

    (J) shelf-life

13. **What scientific technique helps archeologists determine when an organism may have lived?**

    (A) hydrogen bonding

    (B) atomic time

    (C) carbon dating

    (D) blood typing

14. **Which label would _not_ be represented on the periodic table?**

    (F) atomic symbol

    (G) volume

    (H) element

    (J) atomic mass

GO ON

15. **In which of the following does a chemical reaction take place?**

    (A) setting a table

    (B) folding a newspaper

    (C) lighting a match

    (D) riding a bicycle

16. **Which is an example of sublimation?**

    (F) A glass rod melts when placed in a flame.

    (G) A piece of dry ice produces a cloud of gas.

    (H) A drop of water forms on grass in the morning.

    (J) A puddle of water disappears during a hot day.

17. **The opposite of condensation would be _____ .**

    (A) vaporization

    (B) precipitation

    (C) freezing

    (D) percolating

18. **How do you estimate pressure in an equation?**

    (F) divide force by speed

    (G) divide density by volume

    (H) divide force by area

    (J) divide area by volume

19. **As volume decreases, _____ increases.**

    (A) gravity

    (B) balance

    (C) density

    (D) pressure

20. **Salt water is denser than fresh water. Salt water also has a higher boiling point than fresh water. Which type of water produces a greater buoyant force?**

    (F) saltwater, because it is denser

    (G) freshwater, because it is less dense

    (H) saltwater, because it has a higher boiling point

    (J) freshwater, because it has a lower boiling point

21. **Dividing distance by time will help you estimate _____ .**

    (A) acceleration

    (B) speed

    (C) density

    (D) displacement

Name_____   Date_____

Grade 8 Posttest

22. **Which of the following is the clearest example of Newton's third law of motion?**

    (F) A skydiver quickly accelerates to over 100 mph.

    (G) A person not wearing a seatbelt slides forward when the car slows down.

    (H) A coffee cup pushes down on a table with the same force the table pushes up on the cup.

    (J) A car engine becomes very hot as its parts move and rub against one another.

23. **Kyauk tosses a ball in the air and, four seconds later, catches it in the same spot from which she tossed it. Which of the following did not change about this ball?**

    (A) the distance it traveled from 0 to 4 seconds

    (B) its overall displacement from 0 to 4 seconds

    (C) its speed between 0 and 4 seconds

    (D) its velocity between 0 and 4 seconds

24. **What word is used to describe the repeating pattern of atoms within a mineral?**

    (F) spherical

    (G) nuclear

    (H) crystalline

    (J) sedimentary

25. **Why are fungi unable to go through photosynthesis?**

    (A) They have cell walls.

    (B) They lack chlorophyll.

    (C) They are not plants.

    (D) They lack leaves.

26. **A flower has two possible alleles for its color. The dominant allele, R, makes a flower red, while the recessive allele, r, makes it white. Which of the following combinations of alleles will make a flower red?**

    (F) rr only

    (G) Rr only

    (H) RR only

    (J) RR or Rr

27. **A bullfrog starts its life from an egg that hatches into a larva or tadpole stage. After a certain period of time, the tadpole changes into the adult frog. This particular life cycle is known as _____ .**

    (A) decomposition

    (B) transmutation

    (C) complete metamorphosis

    (D) incomplete metamorphosis

28. **An antelope grazes on lush grasses on the African plains. The grass would occupy which level of the food chain?**

    (F) primary consumer

    (G) secondary consumer

    (H) decomposer

    (J) producer

GO ON

Published by Frank Schaffer Publications. Copyright protected.   89   0-7696-8068-2—*Science Test Practice*

29. **Which of the following parts of an ecosystem would be considered abiotic?**

Ⓐ a killer whale

Ⓑ a painted turtle

Ⓒ a willow tree

Ⓓ a mud puddle

30. **When musk oxen feel threatened by a pack of wolves, they instinctively move into a small, tight circle with their calves in the middle and the adults all facing outward. This behavior would be an example of a(n) _____ .**

Ⓕ adaptation

Ⓖ mutation

Ⓗ synapse

Ⓙ biosphere

31. **Which of the following is true about the theory of evolution?**

Ⓐ If an animal learns how to respond to commands its offspring will most likely be born with the same ability.

Ⓑ If an animal runs too slowly to catch enough prey, its offspring will most likely be born with the ability to run faster.

Ⓒ An animal with characteristics better suited to its environment will survive and reproduce better than other animals without that characteristic.

Ⓓ A trait can become common in a population regardless of whether or not that trait increases an animal's chance of survival.

32. **Which process best explains how sedimentary rocks form?**

Ⓕ Volcanoes erupt.

Ⓖ Sediments are pressed together.

Ⓗ Sediments freeze.

Ⓙ Minerals are pulled apart.

33. **Which cycle in nature is the most common way for pollution to move through the environment?**

Ⓐ the sunspot cycle

Ⓑ the water cycle

Ⓒ the lunar cycle

Ⓓ the rock cycle

34. **The location of a jet stream can often be detected by the presence of which long, thin clouds?**

Ⓕ cumulus

Ⓖ stratus

Ⓗ cirrus

Ⓙ altostratus

35. **From inward to outward, which is the correct order of the following parts of the Earth?**

Ⓐ lower mantle, lithosphere, asthenosphere

Ⓑ lower mantle, asthenosphere, lithosphere

Ⓒ asthenosphere, lower mantle, lithosphere

Ⓓ lithosphere, lower mantle, asthenosphere

GO ON

36. What allows Earth to hold on to the sun's heat?

   F Earth's interior
   G Earth's atmosphere
   H Earth's rock cycle
   J Earth's land surfaces

37. On Earth, water and air in the Northern Hemisphere appear to move to the right, but in the Southern Hemisphere, water and air move to the left. This phenomenon can be explained by _____ .

   A evolution theory
   B plate tectonics
   C the Coriolis effect
   D the Barnett effect

38. Genetics is the study of _____ .

   F fossil age
   G bone density
   H heredity
   J evolution

39. Which division of geologic time do scientists believe is the oldest?

   A Mesozoic
   B Precambrian
   C Paleozoic
   D Cenozoic

40. Which event is an example of a scientific prediction?

   F Professor Waddel dropped her cup of tea.
   G Professor Waddel saw clouds outside and grabbed her umbrella.
   H Professor Waddel slipped on the wet pavement.
   J Professor Waddel called out to one of her students.

41. The progression from the thinking that the world was flat to the knowledge that the world is round is an example of _____ .

   A the theory of natural selection
   B the evolution of a theory
   C a scientific prediction
   D a scientific hypothesis

42. The force that holds Earth and other planetary objects in the sun's orbit is referred to as _____ .

   F electrical current
   G magnetic force
   H gravitational pull
   J centrifugal force

GO ON

ANSWER KEY

Page 9
1. C
2. F
3. B
4. J
5. C
6. H

Page 10
7. A
8. H
9. C
10. J
11. A
12. J
13. C
14. H

Page 11
15. B
16. J
17. C
18. F
19. D
20. F
21. C

Page 12
22. H
23. D
24. F
25. A
26. F
27. D
28. H
29. A

Page 13
30. F
31. B
32. G
33. D
34. J
35. D
36. J
37. B
38. J

Page 14
39. A
40. G
41. D
42. F
43. B
44. G
45. B
46. F

Page 15
1. disposal alert
2. biological hazard
3. thermal safety
4. sharp object safety
5. electrical safety
6. fume safety
7. clothing protection safety
8. eye safety
9. chemical safety
10. Don't touch anything, and inform your teacher immediately.
11. Stop, drop, and roll.
12. Run water over the affected skin for at least 15 minutes.
13. Other students should avoid contact with her blood, and inform the teacher immediately. An adult should wear latex gloves to clean up any blood at your lab area. The gloves and paper towels or other cleaning materials should go in a biohazardous waste bag or in a regular trash bag with a biohazard sticker on it.
14. Pull them off inside out so as to avoid touching the areas exposed to hazardous chemicals.

Page 16
1. She will ask the singer which wall made the band sound quietest.
2. The independent variable is the type of insulation.
3. The dependent variable is the level of noise coming from each wall.
4. Possible answer: The garage wall next to the house is almost certainly thicker than the other walls, so it may muffle the sound best regardless of experimental insulation. The singer is not included in the analysis, even though she adds to the noise of the band. The singer knows which insulation is on which wall and may pick the one she expects to work best.
5. Possible answers include cost, difficulty of installation, and appearance of the insulation.
6. Kate will probably muffle the inside garage wall with the best insulation and ask her parents whether that muffles the sound enough for them.

Page 17
1. one
2. light
3. light level
4. seed germination
5. in the closet
6. highest
7. light
8. medium
9. hypothesize
10. sprout
11. bar graph
12. germination
13. seeds
14. light

Page 18
1. C
2. G
3. A
4. H
5. B
6. H
7. C
8. F

Page 19
1. Eyepiece: contains magnifying lenses you look through
2. Arm: supports the body tube
3. Low-power objective: contains the lens with the lowest power magnification
4. Stage clips: hold the microscope slide in place
5. Fine adjustment: sharpens the image under high magnification
6. Coarse adjustment: focuses the image under low power
7. Body tube: connects the eyepiece to the revolving nosepiece
8. Revolving nosepiece: holds and turns the objectives into viewing position
9. High-power objective: contains the lens with the highest magnification
10. Stage: supports the microscope slide
11. Light source: provides light that passes upward through the diaphragm, specimen, and lenses
12. Base: supports the microscope

Page 20
1. C
2. J
3. B
4. H
5. B

Page 21
1. Streams change over time. More data points provide a truer picture.
2. The measurements will change over the course of the day. For instance, the water will be warmer in late afternoon than in the morning.
3. A computer program can help them predict future levels because it can generate a mathematical equation based on the data that has already been collected. Using this equation, future numbers can be calculated.
4. The students sampling water near the mine will find a lower pH, perhaps as low as 2.
5. Bacteria breaking down the dead branches will lower the levels of dissolved oxygen, leaving less oxygen for the fish to breathe, so the fish population will decrease.

Page 22
1. A
2. H
3. B
4. H

Page 23
1. More foxes means fewer rabbits.
2. The fox population will go down because the foxes have fewer rabbits to eat.
3. The rabbit population will increase because there will be less foxes to eat the rabbits.
4. Sound travels more quickly in warmer air.
5. Molecules move more quickly in warmer air and collide more often, so they can transmit a sound wave more rapidly.
6. The echo will return most quickly in the summer and least quickly in the winter.

Page 24
1. D
2. H
3. C

Page 25
1. Possible answer:
   Microscopic examination of ulcered stomach tissue from "many" people.
   Observation that half of samples contained an unknown bacterium.
   Observation that tissue near bacteria was inflamed (red and swollen)
   On basis of observation, more tissue samples were almost always examined.
   Result was that ulcer and bacteria were almost always together.
   Bacterium was identified as Helicobacter pylori.
   Hypothesis that ulcers were caused by Helicobacter pylori was tested on one of the investigators when he swallowed the bacteria.
   Result was that bacteria caused the inflammation, which was the same as that seen with ulcers.

Page 26
1. C
2. G
3. Students' answers should develop a plan to help conserve resources and/or limit population growth, particularly in overcrowded areas.

Page 27
1. D
2. J
3. B
4. F
5. B
6. F
7. D

Page 28

1. Answers will vary, but students should express an understanding that hot air collected in the envelope results in a change in density that allows the balloon to rise due to the buoyant force of less dense air. Escaping hot air from the valve lowers the temperature in the envelope and causes the balloon to drop. To move horizontally, the balloon must be moved by the force of air currents.

Page 29

1. Answers will vary, but students should identify the glass bowl and the metal bowl as floating objects and the glass dish as the sinking object. Students should express an understanding of buoyancy and the buoyant force of objects that contain a large amount of air versus objects that contain little or no air.

Page 30

1. Possible answer: Benefits: produces a high amount of energy, relatively safe, technology will improve the safety of the energy source, produces less radioactive waste than coal plants; Risks: produces radiation, has the ability to make people very ill. Students should also state their opinion about whether they agree or disagree with the mayor's decision.

Page 31

1. Responses will vary, but may address allergic reactions, difficulty with digestion, and contaminants; effects on the environment may include sickness in organisms unaccustomed to the new strain, which may in turn affect humans; students may also discuss lack of knowledge about the effects of GMOs as a problem; to maintain consumer awareness, students may suggest providing information such as brochures in grocery stores, applying labels to genetically modified foods, conducting surveys, holding seminars, and so on.

Page 32

1. B
2. J
3. C
4. H
5. C

Page 33

1. matter
2. molecules
3. liquid
4. solid
5. dissolve
6. solubility
7. increases

Page 34

1. B
2. H
3. D
4. G
5. C
6. J

Page 35

1. Possible answer: This fire was probably not the result of any human activity. It was most likely caused by a lightning strike. This season's weather has been categorized by heat, drought, and high winds. All of these factors make the land more vulnerable to fire. Many animals perished and the land is extremely damaged. However, now the land is ready for new growth. The soil will become more fertile, and new grasses will slow erosion in the watersheds. There are also more dead trees for birds to nest. The dead trees are still standing, but after ten years, new trees will grow amongst the dead. The grass will be more nutritious and will bring more elk to graze. Species of plants and animals will colonize again. With a fresh start, the land will become less susceptible to fire.

Page 36

1. Answers will vary. Students may arrange substances according to color, edibility, viscosity, natural or man-made, toxic or non-toxic, etc. The table should show distinct groups according to the student's ability to sort. All similar substances should be assigned the same symbol and arranged together on the table.
2. Possible answer: Group 18 elements are the noble gases. These gases are found in nature as uncombined elements. They tend not to combine or react with other elements.

Page 37

1. B
2. H
3. C
4. G
5. D
6. H

Page 38

1. fifteen miles
2. The graph should read as follows: the bear's line will go up steeply at the beginning, then go down; the horse's line will go up at the beginning, but not as steeply as the bear's, then it will not go down. It will never get as high as the bear's did at the beginning.
3. the direction the bear was running
4. The line representing the racehorse should rise rapidly to 30 mph and stay there throughout the race. The line representing the bear should rise rapidly to 30 mph and then steadily decline, showing the bear losing his early burst of speed.

Page 39

1. C
2. 0.2 km/h
3. The graph should depict the amount of time required to travel the distance over each of the four phases.

Page 40

1. projectile
2. trajectory
3. force
4. velocity
5. push
6. accelerate
7. gravity
8. motion
9. unbalanced
10. angle

Page 41

1. ability to do work
2. sunlight
3. The skateboard's potential energy becomes kinetic energy and heat energy.
4. at the highest point of its path, when it is not moving
5. Energy can take the form of light, heat, sound, chemical energy, or mechanical energy.
6. Sound waves transmit energy by moving air molecules back and forth in compressional waves.
7. Light waves can move through a vacuum; they do not require air to travel. They are electromagnetic rather than mechanical waves.
8. The water molecules in steam have absorbed more energy. They are farther apart and faster moving than molecules in cool water.
9. joules
10. As the molecules absorb energy, they begin to move more quickly. When one molecule bumps into another, it transfers energy to the molecule it bumped into.

Page 42

1. exothermic
2. endothermic
3. Accept any answer that mentions loss of oxygen.
4. exothermic

Page 43

1. reflection
2. reflecting
3. refracting
4. identical, or the same
5. refracted
6. speed OR direction is acceptable
7. angle
8. reflect

Page 44

Students should draw a diagram in which two light bulbs are connected along the path of the electric current. There should be only one current connecting the batteries and the light bulbs. In the diagram, there should be two batteries; the negative end of one battery should be connected to the positive end of the other. The switch in the circuit should be open.

Page 45

1. A
2. G
3. B
4. G

Page 46

1. Because it is a straight line, the edge of the cover slip is the easiest part of a microscope slide to focus on. Once you have focused on the top of the cover slip, you can find your specimen by moving gradually closer to the slide.
2. the lens that produces the smallest magnification
3. cell membrane, cytoplasm, vacuoles, and nucleus

Page 47

The Venn diagram should be filled in as follows:

Bacteria: move using flagella; Plants: photosynthesize; single-celled: Animals: carry oxygen in blood; multi-cellular; Plants and Animals: have specialized cells; Plants, Bacteria, and Animals:

alive, capable of movement, take in nutrients, excrete wastes

Page 48
1. water
2. mitochondria
3. oxygen
4. carbon dioxide
5. calcium
6. muscle
7. division
8. single-celled
9. reproduce
10. division, or mitosis
11. replicate
12. chromosomes
13. nucleus
14. 46
15. two
16. identical
17. 1–2
18. sexually
19. sperm
20. sexual reproduction
21. diversity

Page 49
1. skeletal
2. heart
3. smooth
4. epithelial
5. cuboidal
6. columnar
7. absorb
8. connective
9. energy
10. red
11. white
12. clots
13. neurons
14. brain
15. electrical

Page 50
1. A
2. F
3. A
4. J
5. A
6. H
7. C
8. F

Page 51
1. D
2. H
3. A
4. J
5. D
6. G
7. B

Page 52
1. Photosynthesis is the opposite of respiration. The substances needed for respiration are the products of photosynthesis, and the substances produced by respiration are needed to begin photosynthesis.
2. light energy from the sun
3. oxygen and water
4. glucose and oxygen
5. They produce food using carbon dioxide and the

energy in chemicals from the vents.

Page 53
1. fertilization
2. female
3. egg
4. sperm
5. gamete
6. n
7. zygote
8. cells
9. 2n
10. 46
11. mitosis
12. meiosis
13. chromosome
14. Possible answers: follow a healthy diet, exercise regularly, remain active
15. Legally, adulthood is based on the age at which a person can do certain activities. However, although puberty ends around age 14, physical and mental changes occur throughout adulthood. It is difficult to say when a person has officially grown up.

Page 54
1. D
2. J
3. D
4. J
5. A
6. G
7. A
8. H

Page 55
1. 4 (all of them)
2. The parent flowers are both homozygous. The offspring are all heterozygous.
3. Students should draw a Punnett square with a cross between "Pp" and "Pp." The resulting genotypes from this cross should be: PP (upper left), Pp (lower left), Pp (upper right), and pp (lower right).
4. 3
5. 2
6. If half the offspring are white, the purple-flowered parent plant must have been heterozygous for flower color (genotype Pp). If it had been homozygous (PP), then all the offspring would have been purple.

Page 56
7. 50%
8. 25%
9. He has a 50% chance of developing Huntington's.
10. Because Huntington's doesn't cause symptoms until adulthood, people who carry the gene live long enough to have children.

Page 57
1. The sparrow's song is learned because if it were inherited, the sparrow would sing the same song regardless of its environment.
2. Beginning to ignore the flowers is a learned behavior. The resemblance of the flowers to female wasps is an inherited behavior; the plants have evolved this appearance because it aids their pollination. The wasps' desire to mate with an object with a particular appearance may be either an inherited or a learned behavior.
3. It is most likely an inherited trait because dogs of the same breed have more similar genes than dogs of different breeds. Most dogs with similar genes take the same amount of time. If it were a learned trait, the length of time wouldn't be affected by breed.
4. Adopted children are raised by parents from whom they did not inherit traits, so they make it easier to sort out which traits are primarily learned and which are primarily inherited.

Page 58
1. D
2. F
3. B

Page 59
1. Decomposers
2. third-level (or tertiary)
3. The producers in this ecosystem are grasses, shrubs, and trees. The consumers are giraffes, zebras, impalas, lions, and cheetahs. The giraffes, zebras, and impalas are herbivores. The lions and cheetahs are carnivores. There are no omnivores described in this scenario.

Page 60
1. Students should draw a food web: The prickly pear cactus should be at the bottom of the web; two arrows should extend from the prickly pear cactus, one should point to the rat and the other should point to the pocket mouse; two arrows should extend from the rat, one should point to the hawk and the other should point to the coyote; three arrows should extend from the pocket mouse, one should point to the

hawk, one to the rattle snake and one to the coyote; one arrow should extend from the rattlesnake and point to the hawk.
2. prickly pear cactus
3. rats, pocket mice, rattlesnakes, coyotes, red-tailed hawks

Page 61
1. Possible answers: The plants grow best in warm weather. A sudden drop in temperature could damage the crops. The insects and the snake are usually active only in warm weather. They would probably seek out shelter if the temperature drops and will no longer be part of the food chain. Without the insects, the birds and meadow voles could go without food for a short time.
2. Possible answers: The cabbage butterflies are dependent on the shade for shelter. The snake needs to bask in the sun to stimulate her appetite. The plants need sun, water, and nutrients from the soil in order to grow. All the animals need oxygen from the air. Plants need carbon dioxide from the air.
3. The swallows, the snake, and the meadow vole are all predators. To remove swallows or voles from the garden will increase the population of insects, which in turn would damage the crops. To remove the snake would increase the population of voles, then decrease the population of insects, and then lead to less damage to the crops.

Page 62
1. A
2. H
3. D
4. The producers in the ocean environment provide food, or energy, for the consumers. If these organisms were removed, the first-level consumers would have no food to eat and decrease in number. This would then begin a cycle that would cause the population of all the consumers living in the ecosystem to decrease.
5. In any ecosystem, energy is passed along from the producers, to the consumers, to the decomposers. Energy is passed through a cycle.

  0-7696-8068-2—*Science Test Practice*

Producers, in an ocean ecosystem, use sunlight to perform photosynthesis. During this process, producers convert sunlight into sugars. When a consumer eats a producer, this energy is passed along. So sunlight is important to an ecosystem because it provides the energy that the organisms need to survive.

Page 63
1. Antigens are substances that cause an immune response, but are not necessarily harmful, like pollen. Pathogens cause disease, and often cause an immune response, so they are technically antigens. An example of a pathogen is a virus.
2. Antibodies are made by B cells during an immune response. They search out particular antigens and then attach to them, which helps the body recognize which pathogens to destroy.
3. During an immune system response, macrophages inside your body activate parts of the brain that raise your body's temperature. When your body is hotter it slows the growth of harmful pathogens.
4. Students should indicate that pathogens can be passed through the air, primarily from sneezes; from contaminated objects such as drinking glasses or doorknobs; from direct person-to-person contact; from animals, like ticks; and from food and water that is not cleaned or cooked correctly.

Page 64
1. Possible response: I believe that physical exercise is the most important habit to have a healthy lifestyle. Its effects are not external as much as internal, and that is where body maintenance matters most. In the long run, having a strong heart, lungs, and bones is more important to survival than how you look. Much of hygiene is related to your appearance or how you are seen on the outside. Exercise on a daily basis is essential because it burns calories and keeps you in shape. It is also a great outlet for stress, which can be very damaging to your

health if not addressed. If I had to choose between hygiene and exercise, I would choose exercise.

Page 65
1. Possible response: Boys generally require more calories than girls do. But in this situation the boy also needs more because he is exercising, which burns calories because the body is using up energy.
2. Amino acids are needed to make proteins. Complete proteins, like what you might find in fish or milk, have all the amino acids needed to make proteins. Incomplete proteins, like in plants, don't have enough amino acids, and therefore require you to eat more foods to build proteins.
3. A
4. J
5. C
6. G

Page 66
1. B
2. J
3. C
4. H
5. A
6. The body has many ways to cool itself down naturally. Sweating, increased blood flow to the skin, and fanning oneself are all ways that the body can cool down without the use of air conditioning.

Page 67
1. D
2. J
3. D
4. H
5. Hibernation is a period during which animals are dormant, or inactive. It is a way to adapt for animals to adapt and survive in a particular climate. It is usually caused by cold temperatures and a lack of food. Animals hibernate in different ways. The length of hibernation may depend on the type of animal, as well as the conditions of the environment.

Page 68
1. B
2. J
3. A
4. H

Page 69
1. C
2. G
3. B
4. H

Page 70
1. The trilobite dies and sinks to the sea floor. In a short amount of time, only the shell remains.
2. The trilobite slowly becomes covered with silt and sand until it is several feet beneath the surface. The layers of sediment build and protect the shell from damage.
3. The chemicals in the shell change and the shell begins to decay. Water begins to flow through the shell, replacing the chemicals with rock-like minerals.
4. C
5. G
6. D
7. J

Page 71
1. Lithosphere
2. Crust
3. Mantle
4. Outer Core
5. Inner Core
6. C
7. H
8. D

Page 72
1. the theory that the Earth's surface (lithosphere) is divided into plates that move around (on top of the asthenosphere)
2. The theory of continental drift is that continents can drift apart from one another and have done so in the past. Pangaea is the single landmass (super-continent) that is thought to have been made up of all the continents before they drifted.
3. They push into each other (at convergent boundaries), move away from each other (at divergent boundaries), or slide past each other (at transform boundaries).
4. When two plates come together, they create stress in the rock. Stress in the rock can cause folding, which can form folded mountains. Stress in the rock can also cause faulting, which can form fault-block mountains. Also, when one of the plates moves under the other (in a subduction zone), volcanic mountains can form.
5. The (Pacific and North American) plates move past each other at a transform boundary. The force of their scraping against each other causes earthquakes (at the San Andreas fault).

Page 73
1. crater
2. vent
3. side vent
4. lava flow
5. pipe
6. magma chamber
7. Lava that has flowed from a volcano and cooled quickly usually cools into smooth rocks. Lava that has spewed from the volcano with great force usually cools into rough, jagged rocks with air pockets.
8. Molten lava must be forced out of the Earth and then be cooled by air and ground temperatures before it turns into extrusive rock.
9. As radioactive elements decay, the heat created during the decay process helps to melt rocks deep within Earth.

Page 74
1. A pine tree cannot send roots into hard rock. There must be a pocket of soil or soil-filled cracks in the rock that hold the pine tree and allow it to absorb water.
2. Lichens are one of the first kinds of organisms to grow on rock. They help make the first soil. Oak trees are the last things to grow on what was once bare rock. They don't survive until much soil has been formed. You can see oak trees and lichens together because not all of the surface in the area weathers at the same time or at the same rate.

Page 75
1. Heat and pressure
2. Melting
3. Weathering and Erosion
4. Dinosaur fossils are normally found in sedimentary rock because they are rocks that most often form through a process of layering. Sedimentary rock doesn't go through the intense heat formation of igneous rocks, which would destroy any fossils.
5. A positive example is rock weathering into soil sediments. A negative example would be when people change the landscape in such a way that removes the topsoil and exposes poor soil or bare rock, making it a poor environment for plants.
6. Metamorphic rocks heat up to form a substance called

0-7696-8068-2—*Science Test Practice*

magma. Magma, when it pours out on Earth's surface, is called lava. Then the magma cools and forms crystals. The minerals can form crystals as they cool. As the magma cools, igneous rock is formed. Igneous rock can form above ground, where the magma cools quickly. Or it can form below ground, where the magma cools slowly.

Page 76
1. food chains
2. organic
3. habitat
4. weathering
5. profile
6. leafy
7. topsoil
8. bedrock
9. proportion
10. loam

Page 77
1. water storage OR ocean or lake
2. evaporation
3. condensation
4. precipitation
5. ground water
6. surface runoff
7. Possible answer: A water molecule in the ocean evaporates into the sky as water vapor as the air temperature warms up. Once in the sky, the atmosphere stores the water molecule in a gaseous state until the temperature drops. At this point, the molecule condenses into a cloud of ice crystals.
8. Possible answer: Surface water runoff can cause many problems with a water supply. As surface water runs into streams and rivers, it can carry fertilizers and pesticides to wherever it drains. Water that flows from roadways may contain pollutants such as oil and antifreeze. Also, waste products from livestock and pets can be carried into water bodies. These problems can be prevented by using non-toxic alternatives to fertilizers and pesticides, keeping livestock away from bodies of water, and disposing of oil and other pollutants properly.

Page 78
1. A
2. J
3. B
4. G
5. D
6. G
7. C

Page 79
1. Thunderstorms are associated with cumulonimbus clouds, which form when the air near the ground is warm and humid. This condition is most common in the summer, when the land heats up.
2. Warm air becomes moist when water evaporates from the surface of the Pacific Ocean. The prevailing winds in North America are from west to east, so the warm, moist air is blown east. As it hits the sides of the mountains, it rises and meets the cooler air above it. The drop in temperature causes the water vapor to condense, and it rains. By the time the prevailing winds have blown that air over the mountains and to the plains, it has dropped most of its water.
3. The cool summer air carries less water vapor, so there are not many water vapor molecules or condensed water droplets to make the air hazy. The result is very clear air. However, Bar Harbor is on the ocean, so there is plenty of water to evaporate. When the air is saturated with water vapor, it condenses into the water droplets that make up the fog.

Page 80
1. Deep currents can cause cooler climates in areas in which they upwell.
2. Answers will vary, but should indicate understanding of the fact that surface currents can cause warmer climates at high latitudes and cooler climate at low latitudes.

Page 81
1. inner
2. Venus
3. Earth
4. Photos
5. Deimos
6. rock
7. outer
8. Ganymede
9. Saturn
10. Titan
11. Uranus
12. Neptune
13. Pluto
14. Charon

Page 82
1. stars
2. hydrogen
3. helium
4. radiation
5. convection
6. photosphere
7. chromosphere
8. 2 million
9. winds
10. dark
11. solar activity
12. 11 years
13. permanent
14. rotation
15. quickly
16. month
17. magnetic
18. prominences
19. solar flares
20. x-rays
21. maximum
22. coronal
23. ejection
24. ionize
25. aurora

Page 83
1. A
2. F
3. B
4. F
5. A
6. H
7. D

Page 84
1. A
2. G
3. B
4. F
5. Waxing gibbous
6. Waning gibbous
7. New
8. Waxing crescent
9. lst quarter

Page 85
1. C
2. J
3. D
4. G
5. D
6. J
7. D

Page 86
1. B
2. H
3. D
4. F
5. C
6. J
7. D

Page 87
8. H
9. B
10. G
11. C
12. H
13. C
14. G

Page 88
15. C
16. G
17. A
18. H
19. D
20. F
21. B

Page 89
22. H
23. B
24. H
25. B
26. J
27. C
28. J

Page 90
29. D
30. F
31. C
32. G
33. B
34. H
35. B

Page 91
36. G
37. C
38. H
39. B
40. G
41. B
42. H

 0-7696-8068-2—*Science Test Practice*